PASS
Cambridge
BEC Vantage

An examination preparation course
Updated for the revised exam

PRACTICE TESTS

with audio CD and Answer key

Russell Whitehead
Michael Black

Introduction

The Cambridge Business English Certificate

The Cambridge Business English Certificate (BEC) is an international Business English examination which offers a language qualification for learners who use, or will need to use, English for their work. It is available at three levels: Preliminary, Vantage and Higher.

The Cambridge BEC Vantage Examination

The Cambridge BEC Vantage examination is made up of four tests.

Reading (60 minutes)

There are five reading tasks. They test skills such as reading for gist and detail, understanding text structure, and knowledge of vocabulary and grammatical structure.

Writing (45 minutes)

There are two writing tasks. The first tests your ability to write concisely, for example, in order to give instructions or request information. The second, longer task, tests your ability to process information and respond appropriately, for example, explaining, summarising, recommending, persuading.

Listening (approximately 40 minutes)

There are three parts, with a total of six tasks. These test your ability to understand monologues and dialogues by completing notes of specific information; identifying topic, function, opinion, etc; and interpreting explanations, arguments and opinions.

Speaking (14 minutes)

The speaking test includes conversation, a mini-presentation and a discussion, with an examiner and another candidate.

Pass Cambridge BEC Vantage Practice Tests

This Practice Test book (and CD) aims to provide useful support for students preparing to take the Cambridge BEC Vantage examination. It consists of:

- **Three complete practice tests**: each practice test includes the Reading, Writing, Listening and Speaking tests and advice on how to approach each task.

- **Preparation**: two pages before each practice test to enable students to check their knowledge and focus on key skills for the test.

- **Tapescripts**: the content of the Listening tests.

- **Answer key**: answers to all the Reading and Listening tests and sample answers for the Writing test.

Recommended approach

We recommend you work through the tests in order. Before you start each test, complete the activities in each Preparation section. You may find it useful to keep a record of useful words, phrases and grammatical structures you come across.

Pass Cambridge BEC Vantage Practice Tests

Preparation

Working out the meaning: Prefixes and suffixes

You can find clues to a word's meaning within the word itself. You should also use your knowledge of the real world to help you work out the likely meaning.

Many words come from the same basic form (or root), e.g. *local, locally, locate, relocate, dislocate, localise, location, locality* all come from the Latin *locus* (= place). As well as the basic form, each of these words contains

- a prefix (*re-, dis-*) which modifies the meaning, or
- a suffix (*-al, -ate, -tion, -ity, -ise*) which may modify the meaning, or identify the word as an adjective, adverb, verb or noun.

Try to identify the basic form and any prefix or suffix. They may help you to work out a word's meaning and grammatical function.

❶ List some words which are related to each of these basic forms.

1 produce
   product, produce, production, productive, producer, productivity, etc
2 employ
   employee, employer, employment, employable, unemployed, unemployment
3 compete
   competitor, competition, competitive, competent, competence
4 consume
   consumer, consumption, consuming, consumable, consumptive
5 differ
   different, difference, differential, differentiate, differentiation

❷ Fill each gap with a word formed from the one in brackets.

1 One way of raising ___*productivity*___ is to reduce costs while maintaining output. (PRODUCE)
2 Several new ___*employees*___ have been taken on in the sales department. (EMPLOY)
3 Our costs are so much higher than those of our rivals that our products are very___*uncompetitive*___. (COMPETE)
4 Cars, televisions and other long-lasting items are known as ___*consumer*___ durables. (CONSUME)
5 Packaging is one way of ___*differentiating*___ one product from another. (DIFFER)

Grammar practice

❶ Complete the sentences with the correct form of the words in brackets, plus any other words you need. This will help you to write more accurately.

1 I look forward to _____*hearing*_____ from you. (HEAR)
2 Few people mind _~~being~~ asked to_ wait, if they are given an explanation. (BE ASKED)
3 It is not worth _spending_ much money on this project. (SPEND)
4 We are trying _to make it easier_ for our sales staff to respond to customers quickly. (MAKE EASIER)
5 As for raw materials, we expect _prices to_ rise by 5% in the coming year. (PRICES)
6 We are committed _to providing cust. with_ exceptional service. (PROVIDE CUSTOMERS)
7 We would _appreciate it if_ you could let us know as soon as possible. (APPRECIATE)
8 The recent trend _for comp. to merge_ is slowing down. (COMPANIES MERGE)
9 The new supervisor seemed _to have left_ his previous job unexpectedly. (LEAVE)
10 We would like _you to_ send us a copy of your certificates. (YOU)

❷ Fill in each gap with one word. This will help you to notice how connections between sentences can be shown, for example in Reading Parts Two and Four, and to improve your writing.

Your CV (or résumé, as it's called in the USA) gives a potential employer their first impression of you. Having seen (1) _it_, they'll decide whether or not to invite (2) _you_ to an interview.

There are several points to bear in mind when writing your CV. Perhaps the most important (3) _one_ is that you should remember what you are trying to achieve. This is to be invited for an interview. If your CV is disorganised and untidy, the reader might assume that you are, too. Presentation – how your CV looks – is important, as well as what you include in it.

(4) _Another_ point is that showing you are right for the job is not enough. You (5) _also_ need to stand out from the other applicants. This doesn't mean that you should write your CV on a balloon, or do any of the other strange things that people sometimes do to get attention. (6) _It_ does mean, though, that you should show that you have thought about the company you are applying to, and about the qualities they might be looking for in the applicants.

(7) _These_ might include an ability to work in a team, for instance. You can demonstrate that ability, even if you haven't had any work experience, by the fact that you belong to a sports team or a club committee, or have helped to organise an event. Most people include all their selling points. (8) _Some, others_ though, do not, for fear of seeming to be showing off.

PRACTICE TEST 1: READING

PART ONE
Questions 1 – 7

How to approach Reading Test Part One
- In this part of the Reading Test you match seven statements with four short texts.
- First read each short text and then read the sentences to see which ones refer to the text.
- Make sure you read each text for overall meaning. Do not choose an answer just because you can see the same words in the text.

- Look at the sentences below and the information about mergers and takeovers involving four companies on the opposite page.
- Which company (**A, B, C** or **D**) does each sentence **1 – 7** refer to?
- For each sentence **1 – 7**, mark one letter (**A, B, C** or **D**) on your Answer Sheet.
- You will need to use some of the letters more than once.

Example:

0 This company expects to benefit from changes in the rules governing mergers.
(**Answer: A**)

1 This company has changed its attitude towards remaining independent.

2 If this company is taken over, changes are likely to take place in its senior management.

3 This company has renewed its efforts to combine with a competitor.

4 This company wishes to remain independent.

5 An attempt to buy this company depends on whether enough money is made available.

6 This company's current lack of success means that a competitor may try to take it over.

7 This company cannot survive on its own for much longer.

A

JARMIN TRAVEL

Tour operator Jarmin Travel is waiting for its chief executive and finance director to make the final decision before making a formal bid for rival HarmonAir. The two companies tried to merge five years ago, when the deal was blocked by the competition authorities. Since then the regulator has eased the criteria by which any merger would be judged. Competition lawyers say a tie-up would almost certainly be allowed this time, and industry analysts believe that both companies are eager for a merger.

B

BARKWAY

Bus operator Barkway has been hit by stiff competition and dwindling profitability. As a result the company has been forced to scrap its plans to expand overseas and instead will concentrate on growing its existing business. The continuing decline in the company's share price has led to speculation that it may fall prey to one of its rivals. This may well prove wrong, though, as Barkway's founder and chief executive, Kerry Matthews, has persuaded the board to do everything in its power to resist a takeover.

C

MARSHMONT'S

Carolyn Swaine, the former chief executive of coffee shop chain Marshmont's, is trying hard to raise capital for a bid for her old company. Swaine left last year after a series of disagreements over Marshmont's future direction, and several top managers are expected to leave if she succeeds in buying the chain. Although Marshmont's is profitable, it is too small to stay independent for much longer, and even if Swaine takes control, the company will soon have to become part of a larger chain.

D

KESTON

Keston, the respected maker of television programmes, has announced that it has agreed an outline deal to merge with Stardust TV. A year ago, with its profits plunging, Keston faced a strong takeover bid by another of its competitors, but fought hard against it, and has since become more profitable. The company is now convinced, however, that its future success lies in being part of a larger organisation. Both Keston and Stardust have a reputation for producing striking television programmes, and a merger is likely to be beneficial, both creatively and financially.

PART TWO

Questions 8 – 12

> ### How to approach Reading Test Part Two
> - In this part of the Reading Test you read a text with gaps in it, and choose the best sentence to fill each gap from a set of seven sentences.
> - First read the text for the overall meaning, then go back and look for the best sentence for each gap.
> - Make sure the sentence fits both the meaning and the grammar of the text around the gap.

- Read the article on the opposite page about an awards scheme for companies.

- Choose the best sentence from below to fill each of the gaps.

- For each gap **8 – 12**, mark one letter (**A – G**) on your Answer Sheet.

- Do not use any letter more than once.

- There is an example at the beginning, **(0)**.

A It will, in effect, be able to demonstrate that it can go on to become an Established Company of the Year before long.

B In order to win, the company will have achieved success in both spheres, and have the evidence to prove it.

C To achieve this, it will be using a variety of means, including the annual report, presentations, a dedicated website and attendance at specialised exhibitions.

D The judges will also consider the degree to which the company has a well planned and soundly financed strategy for its growth and development.

E At the same time, this structure must not stifle the spirit that led to the company's initial success.

F The innovation has been made in order to recognise the increasingly important part which this factor plays in a company's success.

G The competition, which is now in its tenth year, is designed to encourage excellence in smaller public companies based in this area.

The region's best smaller companies

Once again, readers of this magazine have the chance to vote for the region's best companies. **(0)** *G* The awards will be presented at a dinner in Birmingham on May 17.

The pattern established in the first year, of awards for Best Established Company, Best New Company and Best Entrepreneur, will of course continue. However this year sees a new category, that of Best Communication with Investors. **(8)** ...

The Established Company of the Year will be one whose success has lasted for more than just a couple of months or years. Its share price will be performing above the average for its sector, but that is not the only measurement which will be taken into account. **(9)** ... Above all, the winner will be professionally managed, in a way that deals equally well with good and bad trading conditions.

The New Company of the Year will have gone public last year, but will already have shown its growth and management qualities. **(10)** ... In fact three early winners have already been successful in this second category, as well.

The Entrepreneur of the Year will be someone with a proven track record of expertise in setting up and providing leadership to one or possibly more businesses. He or she will have created an organisation that can deal with the demands placed on it as a public company. **(11)** ... The winner will have maintained a balance between that original energy and the need to adapt as the company grows.

In our new category, Best Communication with Investors, the winning company will show that it is engaging in two-way dialogue with both actual and potential investors. **(12)** ... All of these communication channels will be carefully tailored for the intended audience. In addition, the company is likely to distribute press releases by electronic means, to maximise its opportunities for publicity.

Nominations for awards were invited several months ago, and reduced by the judges to a shortlist of three in each category. The shortlisted companies are described below, together with details of how to vote. Please get your vote to us no later than 31 March.

PART THREE

Questions 13 – 18

> **How to approach Reading Test Part Three**
> - In this part of the Reading Test you read a longer text and answer six questions.
> - First read the questions. Try to get an idea of what the text will be about. Then read the text quickly for general understanding.
> - Then read the text and questions more carefully, choosing the best answer to each question. Do not choose an answer just because you can see the same words in the text.

- Read the article below about a fast-food chain and the questions on the opposite page.

- For each question **13 – 18**, mark one letter (**A**, **B**, **C** or **D**) on your Answer Sheet for the answer you choose.

Turning around a fast-food chain

Sparrow is a well-established fast-food chain, with 200 restaurants run by franchisees, and almost as many company-owned ones. Some years ago, the group to which Sparrow belonged was taken over by another company, which owned a variety of retail businesses. Although demand for a Sparrow franchise showed no sign of declining, overall the chain was in an unhealthy state. Its properties, the majority of them in small towns, needed refurbishment to stand comparison with its competitors. With more and more fast-food concepts reaching the market, the distinctive Sparrow menu had to struggle for attention. And to make matters worse, its new owners had bought it as one of a number of companies, and had no plans to give it the investment it required.

Sparrow stagnated for another two years, until a new chief executive, Carl Pearson, decided to build up its market share. He commissioned a survey, which showed that consumers who already used Sparrow restaurants were overwhelmingly positive about the chain, while customers of other fast-food chains, particularly those selling pizzas or hamburgers, were reluctant to be tempted away from them. Sparrow had to develop a new promotional campaign – one that would enhance the public's perceptions of the chain and set it apart from its competitors.

Pearson faced a battle over the future of the Sparrow brand. The chain's owner now favoured taking Sparrow's outlets upmarket and rebranding them as Marcy's restaurants, one of its other, better known brands. Pearson resisted, arguing for an advertising campaign designed to convince customers that visits to Sparrow restaurants were fun. Such an attempt to establish a positive relationship between a company and the general public was unusual for that time. Pearson strongly believed that numbers were the key to success, rather than customers' spending power. His arguments won the day.

The campaign itself broke some of the fast-food industry's advertising conventions. The television commercials played down traditional product shots – most of its competitors' advertisements had mouth-watering shots of food – and focused instead on entertainment and humour. The usual jingles gave way to spots featuring original songs performed by a variety of stars. Instead of trying to show the superiority of a specific product, the intention was to position Sparrow in the hearts of potential customers.

Pearson hired two advertising agencies to handle this campaign, and spent a considerable time with them, discussing and developing the brief he had outlined. Once that had been agreed in detail, he left them to get on with their work. Instead of dividing responsibilities, as would normally happen when two agencies collaborate, they decided to develop a team concept, with both having equal opportunities for creative input.

Pearson also made other decisions which he believed would contribute to the new Sparrow image. He laid off 400 employees in the headquarters and company field offices, and reduced the management hierarchy. He insisted on uniformity of standards in all restaurants, and warned franchisees that if they ran untidy, unprofitable restaurants, Sparrow would close them, or if necessary, buy them. In addition Sparrow offered to lower the rent of any franchisees who achieved a certain increase in their turnover.

These efforts paid off, and Sparrow soon became one of the most successful fast-food chains in the regions where it operates.

13 According to the first paragraph, what problem did Sparrow face when it was taken over?

    A   Its new owners were uninterested in spending money on it.

    B   Its products were too similar to those of its competitors.

    C   It received few applications from potential franchisees.

    D   It had a number of restaurants which were poorly situated.

14 The survey commissioned by Carl Pearson showed that

    A   Sparrow's existing customers were dissatisfied.

    B   the type of food that Sparrow offered was losing popularity.

    C   people were unwilling to change to Sparrow restaurants.

    D   Sparrow's name was not well known to the general public.

15 According to the third paragraph, what was Pearson's plan for Sparrow?

    A   to attract consumers who had more money to spend

    B   to associate it with a certain type of experience

    C   to make it part of another, more famous brand

    D   to make its restaurants more attractive and up-to-date

16 How were Sparrow's TV advertisements different from those of other fast-food businesses?

    A   They used celebrities to present the products.

    B   There was very little use of music.

    C   They compared the company with its competitors.

    D   There were very few product shots.

17 How was the advertising campaign handled?

    A   The agencies worked together as one unit.

    B   Pearson kept a close eye on the agencies' work.

    C   The agencies focused on different parts of the campaign.

    D   Pearson wrote a full brief before contacting the agencies.

18 According to the sixth paragraph, Pearson decided to

    A   reduce staffing levels in the restaurants.

    B   offer financial incentives to new franchisees.

    C   turn all the restaurants into company-owned outlets.

    D   ensure that all the restaurants were of the same quality.

PART FOUR

Questions 19 – 33

How to approach Reading Test Part Four

- This part of the Reading Test tests your vocabulary.
- Read the whole text quickly to find out what it is about. As you read, try to predict the words that might fill the gaps.
- Next, look at the four possible answers for each gap and cross out any obviously incorrect words.
- Then read both before and after each gap to decide which word should go in it. The word needs to fit both the meaning and the grammar.
- After completing all the gaps, read the whole text again to check your answers.

- Read the article on the opposite page about why some small companies fail to grow.

- Choose the best word to fill each gap from **A, B, C** or **D** below.

- For each question **19 – 33**, mark one letter (**A, B, C** or **D**) on your Answer Sheet.

- There is an example at the beginning (**0**).

Example: (Answer: A)

0	**A** expand	**B** increase	**C** enlarge	**D** broaden
19	**A** condemn	**B** accuse	**C** charge	**D** blame
20	**A** admission	**B** entry	**C** access	**D** entrance
21	**A** currency	**B** money	**C** cash	**D** banknote
22	**A** specify	**B** categorise	**C** identify	**D** allocate
23	**A** achieved	**B** drawn	**C** acquired	**D** obtained
24	**A** clear	**B** distinct	**C** resolved	**D** defined
25	**A** foundation	**B** ground	**C** base	**D** root
26	**A** notified	**B** expressed	**C** informed	**D** addressed
27	**A** caught	**B** occupied	**C** held	**D** contained
28	**A** significance	**B** meaning	**C** definition	**D** sense
29	**A** place	**B** grade	**C** position	**D** stage
30	**A** watching for	**B** looking after	**C** bringing up	**D** waiting on
31	**A** support	**B** aid	**C** contribute	**D** assist
32	**A** avoids	**B** obstructs	**C** prevents	**D** evades
33	**A** over	**B** across	**C** down	**D** along

Why do some small companies **stay** small?

It is often assumed that if a small company fails to (0) ... , it is because of external factors. So it may come as something of a surprise to discover that many small companies have only themselves to (19) ... for their lack of growth. In fact, if you run a small business, you shouldn't waste much time wondering whether you have (20) ... to investment capital; still less, analysing fluctuations in (21) ... exchange rates. You are more likely to (22) ... the main barrier to greater success by looking in the mirror.

This is a conclusion that can be (23) ... from a recent study based on interviews with the owner-managers of 40 small businesses. The research makes the reason (24) ... : management behaviour, however well intentioned, is often the (25) ... of the problem. This was the overwhelming view (26) ... by the managers surveyed: the main barrier to growth was the fact that day-to-day issues (27) ... all their time. The problems that many larger businesses face – lack of funds and insufficient government support – were of relatively minor (28) ... for these small companies.

The survey shows that while owner-managers often work very hard running their business, many never take it on to the next (29) ... . The reason is that they are too busy (30) ... their sales, marketing and finance functions. Limited resources may (31) ... to this, but many owner-managers are unwilling to delegate even insignificant decisions. As a result, without realising it, they create a style of working that (32) ... them from moving forward. One of the most important lessons for managers is learning to let go - very few people can do everything themselves. Instead they need to hire staff able to take (33) ... some of their responsibilities.

PART FIVE

Questions 34 – 45

How to approach Reading Test Part Five

- This part of the Reading Test tests your ability to identify additional or unnecessary words in a text. Most lines contain one extra word which is incorrect.
- Read the whole text quickly to find out what it is about. As you read, try to identify the words that are incorrect. Make sure you consider whole sentences, and not each line separately.
- Then read the text again, and write down the extra words.
- Remember there will be only one extra word in a line, and some lines are correct.

- Read the article on the opposite page about organising events.

- In most of the lines **34 – 45** there is one extra word. It is either grammatically incorrect or does not fit in with the meaning of the text. Some lines, however, are correct.

- If a line is correct, write CORRECT on your Answer Sheet.

- If there is an extra word in the line, write the extra word in CAPITAL LETTERS on your Answer Sheet.

- The exercise begins with two examples, **(0)** and **(00)**.

Example:

0 | T | A | S | K | | | | | |

00 | C | O | R | R | E | C | T | | |

Organising Events

0	First task of all, you need to be sure that an event is really the best way to get your
00	message across to customers. Maybe advertising or direct mail would be more
34	effective instead. While an event involves persuading key people to attend,
35	and can take out a great deal of time and money, so you should think very
36	carefully before choosing that method. If you go for an event, see how soon
37	others do it, and adapt from their ideas to suit your own circumstances. You'll
38	need to produce an event strategy and checklist, and then keep on to it. Make
39	sure your key players agree to look an outline strategy at the start. The smallest
40	things can let you go down, with potentially serious results. This means you
41	should have plans in place in which case speakers arrive late, contractors are
42	unreliable or equipment fails. Keep everyone involved informed of how plans
43	are progressing, to avoid a lack of information is leading to confusion and
44	uncertainty. Form a team and delegate responsibilities. Afterwards, thank to
45	everybody. This is very important: after all, you could well need them again
	next time.

PRACTICE TEST 1: WRITING

PART ONE

How to approach Writing Test Part One
- Part One counts for one third of the total marks in the Writing Test.
- You should spend no more than 15 minutes on Part One.
- You will be asked to write a note, memo, email or message to one or more people in your company.
- The first bullet point of the instructions outlines the situation.
- The second bullet point tells you what you should write, who you are writing it for, and the points that must be included.
- It is best to follow the order of the points that are required, as you will lose marks if you leave out any of them.

Planning
- Read the instructions carefully so that you know what to do, and underline the key words.

Writing
- Express yourself briefly and clearly.
- For a memo or email you don't need to include *to, from, date* or *subject*.
- Try to use a range of appropriate vocabulary and grammatical structures.
- Make the language suitable for the reader(s).

Checking
- After writing, read what you have written, correct mistakes and make improvements. If you want to add anything, use a sign, e.g. *. Put a line through anything you want to omit. Don't rewrite the whole of your answer.
- Make sure the examiner will be able to read your answer. Use a pen and your normal handwriting (do not write in capital letters).
- Check that you have written your answer in 40–50 words.

- You are a director of a manufacturing company. A foreign delegation will soon be visiting the company. You are responsible for supervising arrangements for the visit.
- Write a memo to the office manager of your company:
    - saying when the delegates will arrive
    - explaining what he should show them
    - telling him the arrangements for lunch.
- Write **40 – 50** words.

Memo

To: Jerry Carter
From: Susannah Cowley
Subject: Foreign delegation

PART TWO

How to approach Writing Test Part Two

- Part Two counts for two thirds of the total marks in the Writing Test.
- You should spend about 30 minutes on Part Two.
- You will be asked to write a report, proposal or piece of business correspondence.
- You will be given information, such as a letter, advertisement, or charts and graphs, as the starting point for your answer, and will be told who to write to.
- About five 'handwritten' notes will also be given. You must use all these notes when writing your answer, and will need to invent information in connection with some of them. If you leave out any of the five notes, you will lose marks.

Planning
- Read the instructions carefully so that you know what do, and underline the key words.
- Make an outline plan, putting the five notes into a suitable order.

Writing
- Start your answer by briefly saying why you are writing.
- Express your ideas clearly.
- Try to use a wide range of appropriate vocabulary and grammatical structures.
- For a piece of business correspondence, include suitable openings and closings (e.g. *Dear Ms Smith* and *Yours sincerely* with your signature), but no addresses.
- Do not present a report or proposal in the form of a letter.
- Make the formality of the language suitable for the reader(s).

Checking
- After writing, read what you have written, correct mistakes and make improvements. If you want to add anything, use a sign, e.g. *. Put a line through anything you want to omit. Don't rewrite the whole of your answer.
- Make sure the examiner will be able to read your answer. Use a pen and your normal handwriting (do not write in capital letters).
- Check that you have written your answer in 120–140 words.

- Your company is willing to pay for you to attend a management training course. You have received a leaflet about a suitable course.

- Read the leaflet below, on which you have already made some handwritten notes.

- Then, using all your handwritten notes, write a proposal for your Training Manager, explaining why you would like to attend the course.

- Write **120 – 140** words.

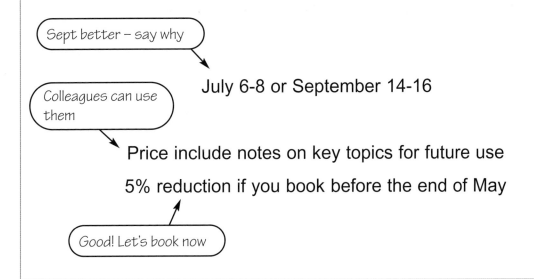

An introduction to management

- Programme includes:

    - Planning and setting objectives
    - Communication skills *Very useful in my job – explain why*
    - Delegating work

- Three-day course

- Maximum 20 participants

- Includes work in small groups *Good way of working*

Sept better – say why

July 6-8 or September 14-16

Colleagues can use them

Price include notes on key topics for future use

5% reduction if you book before the end of May

Good! Let's book now

PRACTICE TEST 1: LISTENING

PART ONE
Questions 1 – 12

How to approach Listening Test Part One
- This part is in three sections. In each section you listen to a telephone conversation or message.
- You will hear each section twice before you hear the next one.
- Before you listen, read the notes. Think about what you are going to hear.
- Note all possible answers as you listen for the first time. Do not make an immediate decision.
- You should write words that you hear without changing them. They must fit the meaning of the notes.
- Decide on your final answer only after you have listened for the second time.
- Check that you have used no more than two words or a number in each numbered space.

- You will hear three telephone conversations or messages.

- Write one or two words or a number in the numbered spaces on the notes or forms.

- You will hear each recording twice.

Conversation One (Questions 1 – 4)

- Look at the form below.

- You will hear a woman phoning a college about a course.

Stangrave & Hoxton College
Faculty of Business

Course details

Name: Sylvia Carlyle

Course accepted for: (**1**) ....

Module A: (**2**) ....

Module B: (**3**) ....

Subject area of term paper: (**4**) ....

Conversation Two (Questions 5 – 8)

- Look at the notes below.

- You will hear a recorded message about a job vacancy.

Notes

Vacancy at Sandridge Centre for (**5**) ....

must know a lot about (**6**) ....

must have carried out (**7**) ....

(**8**) .... knowledge would be a plus

Conversation Three (Questions 9 – 12)

- Look at the form below.

- You will hear a man enquiring about computer workstations.

Moorfield's Department Stores
Workstations department
Enquiry form

Customer: Crawford's

Item: (9) ....

Model: (10) ....

Extra(s): (11) ....

Notes: Also interested in a (12) ....

PART TWO
Questions 13 – 22

How to approach Listening Test Part Two

- This part is in two sections. In each section you listen to five short monologues, spoken by five different speakers. You will hear the first section twice, and then the second section twice.
- For each monologue you must choose one out of eight options.
- First read the task carefully, and make sure that you know what you need to decide.
- Listen for the overall meaning of each monologue. Do not choose an answer just because you hear the same words in the recording as in the question.
- Decide on your final answer only after you have listened for the second time.
- Check that you have not used the same option more than once.

Section One (Questions 13 – 17)

- You will hear five short recordings.

- For each recording, decide what each speaker's goal is for their career.

- Write one letter (**A – H**) next to the number of the recording.

- Do not use any letter more than once.

- You will hear the five recordings twice.

13	**A** to gain promotion to a more responsible position
	B to specialise in a particular aspect of their work
14	**C** to live and work abroad
	D to be recognised as an innovator
15	**E** to go into business on their own
16	**F** to travel on business more often
	G to join another company
17	**H** to start working in a different field

Section Two (Questions 18 – 22)

- You will hear another five recordings.

- For each recording, decide what reason each speaker gives for the problem they mention.

- Write one letter (**A – H**) next to the number of the recording.

- Do not use any letter more than once.

- You will hear the five recordings twice.

18	....	**A**	The company tried to operate in too many markets.
		B	The company's spending priorities were mistaken.
19	....	**C**	Unsuitable staff were appointed.
		D	The company failed to update its products.
20	....	**E**	The company's suppliers were unreliable.
		F	The company used inappropriate retailers.
21	....	**G**	A number of new competitors entered the market.
22	....	**H**	The company set its prices at the wrong levels.

PART THREE

Questions 23 – 30

> **How to approach Listening Test Part Three**
> - In this part you listen twice to a long conversation, interview or monologue, and answer eight questions.
> - Before you listen, read the questions. Think about what will be said.
> - Note all possible answers as you listen for the first time. Do not make an immediate decision.
> - Listen for overall meaning. Do not choose an answer just because you hear the same words in the recording as in the question.
> - Decide on your final answer only after you have listened for the second time.

- You will hear a college lecturer talking to a class of business students about a merger between two supermarket chains.

- For each question **23 – 30**, mark one letter (**A, B** or **C**) for the correct answer.

- You will hear the recording twice.

23 The merger was expected to help the combined company to

    A   reduce its costs.
    B   improve its public image.
    C   compete with the market leaders.

24 One reason given for the merger's lack of success is

    A   difficulties in integrating the two brands' supply chains.
    B   increased competition from other supermarket businesses.
    C   customers' unwillingness to accept changes in the stores.

25 The management structure following the merger led to

    A   interpersonal disagreements.
    B   confusion about responsibilities.
    C   over-staffing at senior levels.

26 The company decided to sell some of its premises in order to

    A   get itself out of debt.
    B   reposition itself in the market.
    C   acquire new types of businesses.

27 The company tries to attract customers by

    A   offering benefits to large spenders.

    B   promoting special offers.

    C   keeping prices low.

28 The Chairman recently blamed the group's poor performance on

    A   lack of customer consultation.

    B   the country's economic situation.

    C   continuing internal problems.

29 The Chairman's plans for improving the company's performance include

    A   introducing high-quality product ranges.

    B   increasing its advertising spend.

    C   assessing its suppliers.

30 The first task which the speaker sets the students is to

    A   analyse the reasons for the merger.

    B   make recommendations concerning the company's future strategy.

    C   consider the company's responses to problems.

PRACTICE TEST 1: SPEAKING

PART ONE: CONVERSATION

How to approach Speaking Test Part One
- In this part of the test you answer questions about yourself and about business topics, and express opinions.
- Before the exam, think of answers to possible questions about your work or studies, business in your country, and a wide range of business-related matters. Below are some questions of the types which you might need to answer.
- In the exam, listen carefully to the questions. Make sure you answer what the examiner asks you. Ask the examiner to repeat a question if necessary. Speak to both the examiner and the other candidate, and listen to what the other candidate says.
- Try to give more than just basic answers, and give examples to show what you mean.
- Remember that you are being tested on your ability to speak in English, not on your knowledge of specific areas of business. If you do not know an answer, say so, and try to speculate.

Practise answering these questions.

What types of business are most successful in your home town?

Which aspects of business interest you most?

What training would you most like to have in the future?

Do you think companies should provide training for all staff?

Is it better to attend a full-time or a part-time training course?

Do it later

PART TWO: INDIVIDUAL MINI-PRESENTATION

How to approach Speaking Test Part Two

- In this part of the test you give a short talk (approximately one minute) on a business topic.
- You choose one of three topics. Each one is in the form of a question beginning *What is important when* … ? There will be two words or phrases to help you develop your ideas, but it isn't essential to use these.
- You have one minute to prepare your ideas. In this time make brief notes to give you a structure and some key words.
- When you talk, make the structure clear, for example by giving a brief introduction and conclusion, and using linking words and phrases to introduce each section.
- Speak to both the examiner and the other candidate, and listen to what the other candidate says. You will have to ask the other candidate a question about their presentation after they have spoken.
- Remember that you are being tested on your ability to speak in English, not on your knowledge of specific areas of business, so if you don't know much about a topic, just say what you can about it.

Practise preparing short talks on the topics below and on the next page.

Task Sheet One

A   WHAT IS IMPORTANT WHEN…?

Interviewing candidates for a job

- Personal qualities
- Qualifications
-
-

B   WHAT IS IMPORTANT WHEN…?

Conducting market research

- Competition
- Characteristics of sample
-
-

C   WHAT IS IMPORTANT WHEN…?

Organising a training programme

- Availability
- Costs
-
-

Task Sheet Two

A   WHAT IS IMPORTANT WHEN...?

Planning a career

- Qualifications
- Future trends
-
-

B   WHAT IS IMPORTANT WHEN...?

Choosing a new supplier

- Product quality
- Costs
-
-

C   WHAT IS IMPORTANT WHEN...?

Delegating tasks

- Priorities
- Previous experience
-
-

PART THREE: DISCUSSION

How to approach Speaking Test Part Three

- In this part of the test you work with the other candidate. The examiner gives you a scenario and a task to discuss. You need to have a serious discussion of the task, with the type of interaction which would be appropriate to a work environment.
- You and the other candidate should try to imagine yourselves in a work environment, faced with a real situation to discuss, on which you should try to reach some decisions.
- You have about 30 seconds to prepare your ideas. Use this time to ensure you understand the task. Ask the examiner to explain anything you are unsure of.
- Listen to the other candidate and respond to what they say. Do not just give your own opinions, or simply agree with the other candidate.
- Try to make more than just basic comments.
- Following your discussion with the other candidate, the examiner will ask you questions on the same topic. Develop your answers, and give examples to show what you mean. Listen to what the other candidate says.

Practise discussing this task and answering the questions that follow.

Trade fair stand

Your company will soon have a stand at a trade fair abroad for the first time.

You have been given the job of organising the stand.

Discuss the situation together, and decide:

- what information and products you will need to provide on the stand
- what staffing requirements the stand will have.

Follow-up questions:

- Have you ever attended a trade fair?
- How useful do you think trade fairs can be in promoting a company's products or services?
- Might there be any problems in attending trade fairs?
- What other means are effective in promoting goods or services?
- Do you think the role of marketing will change in the future?

Preparation

Working out the meaning: Prefixes and suffixes

1 Match each prefix and suffix from the box with its approximate meaning below. Two share the same meaning.

prefixes		
	1 counter-	*counteract, counterbalance, counterproductive*
	2 mal-	*malpractice, malfunction, malformation*
	3 post-	*postdate, postpone, postgraduate*
	4 trans-	*transact, transfer, transform, transit, transport*

suffixes		
	5 -ify	*diversify, simplify, identify, certify*
	6 -ee	*payee, addressee, employee*
	7 -let	*leaflet, booklet, applet*
	8 -en	*lengthen, strengthen, harden, moisten*

approximate meanings

a) across, through

b) to make, to give something (more of) a particular quality

c) after, behind

d) against, opposite, in return

e) bad, badly

f) small

g) someone who receives something, or is the object of an action

Working out the meaning: Compound words

Compound words are ones which consist of two words. The meaning is often a combination of the meanings of the 2 words, e.g. shareholder – a person who holds shares in a company.

2 Match each word with its meaning.

1	bottleneck	a) intense, fierce (e.g. describing competition)
2	cut-throat	b) accumulate goods for future use
3	moonlight	c) constricted place or section of a process
4	stockpile	d) unable to be disproved (e.g. describing an excuse)
5	watertight	e) have a second, part-time job (usually in the evening) in addition to a full-time one.

Grammar practice

❶ Choose the best linking word or phrase of the four alternatives to make the meaning clear. This will help you in Reading Parts Two and Four, and to improve your writing.

After working for Gardener's, a company with a virtual monopoly in the plastic flowers sector, I eventually decided to branch out on my own, and set up Hulme's Blooms twenty years ago. (1) _____ wanting to work independently, my vision was to provide my former employer with stiff competition. As you may know, our success has far exceeded my original expectations.

Today we can boast customers in 17 countries, (2) _____ we face considerable competition in many markets. (3) _____, as a result of our success, we are facing difficulties in the supply of plastic granulate of an appropriate quality, and our production and sales staff are stretched to capacity. (4) _____ strenuous efforts to find new suppliers of plastic granulate, we cannot purchase enough to meet our needs. (5) _____, it is clear that we will continue to face serious problems, (6) _____ we take on extra staff.

1	A Despite	B Besides	C Although	D On the one hand
2	A and	B in spite of	C because	D even though
3	A However	B Although	C Instead	D Moreover
4	A In spite of	B As a result of	C In addition to	D In consequence of
5	A However	B Despite	C In addition	D On the other hand
6	A so	B because	C even if	D although

❷ Join each pair of sentences to form one sentence. Where possible, try to find two answers. This will help you to improve your writing.

1 The old equipment needs to be replaced. It keeps breaking down.
(The old equipment needs to be replaced …)
   … as it keeps breaking down. / … because of its constant breakdowns.

2 Sharman Ltd increased its market share last year. This rose by 2%.
(Sharman Ltd saw …)

_____

3 The conference attracted new delegates. This was interesting.
(What was interesting about the conference …)

_____

4 The company ran an advertising campaign. That's why sales rose by 10%.
(The advertising campaign resulted in …)

_____

5 Effective communication involves listening to what is said. It also involves noticing what is not said.
(Effective communication involves …)

_____

PRACTICE TEST 2: READING

PART ONE

Questions 1 – 7

How to approach Reading Test Part One
- In this part of the Reading Test you match seven statements with four short texts.
- First read each short text and then read the sentences to see which ones refer to the text.
- Make sure you read each text for overall meaning. Do not choose an answer just because you can see the same words in the text.

- Look at the sentences below and the advice for secretaries and personal assistants about dealing with a new manager on the opposite page.

- Which company (**A, B, C** or **D**) does each sentence **1 – 7** refer to?

- For each sentence **1 – 7**, mark one letter (**A, B, C** or **D**) on your Answer Sheet.

- You will need to use some of the letters more than once.

Example:

0 You will probably be pleased with some of the innovations that your new manager introduces
(**Answer: A**)

1 You may be able to explore your career development with your new manager.

2 You may need to point out why certain procedures are in place.

3 Help your new manager to feel relaxed when they take up the position.

4 You should resist taking on extra tasks which you do not consider part of your role.

5 You may need help in settling differences with your new manager.

6 You should not encourage colleagues to become hostile towards your new manager.

7 A new manager may benefit from your knowledge of conventions and attitudes within the company.

A   If you are a secretary, or personal assistant, getting a new manager means that your job will probably change, too. The new person is likely to have different ideas about how things should be done, and you may well find that some of these are changes for the better. But remember that the new manager might be feeling nervous. If you treat their first day in the job as though it's your own first day, too, it will ease the transition for them, and benefit you both.

B   Your new manager may have different ideas from your previous one about personal habits, such as eating at your desk, and you will have to accept that. Their changes may not always be appropriate or helpful, however. It could be that you are asked to open the post later on in the day, when you know that it is important to get it sorted first thing. In this case, rather than grumbling about it and spreading discontent around the office, explain if there is a genuine reason for a particular way of working.

C   If your new manager has joined the company from outside, they will be on a steep learning curve. You can really show your worth by bringing them up to speed on the company history and culture. The appointment of a new manager is also the ideal opportunity for you to discuss your prospects for training and promotion with them, though raising the subject on their first day is unlikely to give them a good impression of you.

D   If you are concerned about changes that your new manager wants to make to your job, first check your job description, if you have one, then speak to him or her calmly about it. If work is being put your way that is someone else's responsibility, say so. Make it clear what you believe to be the limits of your job. Ideally, the two of you will come to an agreement that suits both parties. Failing that, consider contacting the human resources department to see if it can act as mediator.

PART TWO

How to approach Reading Test Part Two
- In this part of the Reading Test you read a text with gaps in it, and choose the best sentence to fill each gap from a set of seven sentences.
- First read the text for the overall meaning, then go back and look for the best sentence for each gap.
- Make sure the sentence fits both the meaning and the grammar of the text around the gap.

Questions 8 – 12

- Read the article on the opposite page about a club for company chairmen and women.
- Choose the best sentence from below to fill each of the gaps.
- For each gap **8 – 12**, mark one letter (**A – G**) on your Answer Sheet.
- Do not use any letter more than once.
- There is an example at the beginning, **(0)**.

A   Currently almost all of them head listed companies – although generally not the biggest – and some come from private companies and the public sector.

B   Among other things, it came down in favour of companies separating the roles of chairman and chief executive.

C   Many also regard the opportunity to test new thinking as a major benefit.

D   Some forum members suspect that many of those in powerful positions think they know it all already.

E   Dividing the decision-making process into parts, each with its own focus, achieved the desired outcome.

F   There are no clear guidelines.

G   His plan was to hold another one at which the issue would be resolved.

A forum for chairmen and women to exchange ideas

When Cadbury Schweppes was considering selling its food and health products businesses in the mid-1980s, Sir Adrian Cadbury, chairman at the time, called a board meeting and told the directors not to make up their minds, but simply to talk about selling the businesses. **(0)** *G* At that first meeting, everyone spoke up. Opinion was divided. The second meeting was different. 'We had a very large degree of agreement,' Sir Adrian says. **(8)** ... He had feared that attempting to deal with the matter just in one meeting would inhibit open discussion.

How to chair a company has been a long-time preoccupation of Sir Adrian's. The committee he headed in the early 1990s – set up by the British government to investigate corporate governance – produced the Cadbury report. **(9)** ... This was just one of its many recommendations, which had a major impact on how companies are managed.

Being chairman is a difficult job, Sir Adrian says. **(10)** ... For that reason, he has helped set up the Chairmen's Forum, a club of like-minded people who get together to exchange ideas and learn how to chair companies. As well as hosting dinners, addressed by major players in the business world, the forum has held seminars to discuss issues such as how to get the best out of the board and how to respond to a crisis.

James Watson, head of the forum's steering committee, believes the organisation should do more to publicise its existence. One of the reasons is that he wants to attract a more diverse group of chairmen and women as the forum increases its size to the 100 members he regards as optimal. **(11)** ... But all are UK-based and the vast majority are male. The forum wants to attract more women and more non-British members to what it believes is the world's only chairmen's club.

Most chairmen of the biggest UK companies have stayed away. **(12)** ... Sir Adrian is more charitable: he believes chairmen of large groups do not have time for forum meetings. But he argues that one should not underestimate how difficult the job is. Chairing any meeting is a challenge. And as Jane Kelly, the first woman to join the organisation, says, leading is often a solitary task. 'The higher up you move in any organisation, the lonelier you can be. At each level, the number of people you can talk to is smaller.' Hence the value of a club like the Chairmen's Forum.

> ### How to approach Reading Test Part Three
> - In this part of the Reading Test you read a longer text and answer six questions.
> - First read the questions. Try to get an idea of what the text will be about. Then read the text quickly for general understanding.
> - Then read the text and questions more carefully, choosing the best answer to each question. Do not choose an answer just because you can see the same words in the text.

- Read the article below about report writing and the questions on the opposite page.

- For each question **13 – 18**, mark one letter (**A**, **B**, **C** or **D**) on your Answer Sheet for the answer you choose.

Report writing: a growing demand

Writing reports is an essential business skill, one which is often thought to be quite distinct from those required for letter writing and speech making, for instance, yet in each case success comes from taking a common basic approach. Nowadays, the availability of computers makes it tempting to devote much of the planning stage of writing a report to experimenting with graphics and layout – which may well benefit the reader – but we risk focusing on presentation at the expense of substance. After all, the absence of visible corrections may not mean an absence of errors.

Skill at report writing is needed for anything from a short magazine article to a lengthy submission to a public enquiry. In business, it is not only required for more and more jobs; it can also make a difference to your chances of promotion. When you speak, people know that you don't have the time to organise your ideas, or choose the right words. But when you write, they assume you've got the time, and expect better organisation, more careful expression. And – worryingly, perhaps, for many – they may read your words several times.

The increasing importance of reports reflects changes in the workplace. Gone are the days when businesses or departments were small enough for decisions to be taken after a discussion between the manager and a specialist on the shop floor. Companies and organisations have expanded and are now increasingly dependent on documentation. This provides a record of decisions taken, and evidence that the issues have been analysed. Effective reports can enable management to retain the confidence of shareholders, directors and bankers.

Some reports, like the minutes of a meeting, record the main points of discussions, any decisions made and advice given. They also have one eye on the future. Lawyers and other professionals file reports as a record of their contact with clients. These are then available for future reference and for consultation by colleagues if necessary. A report filed at the time is considered an accurate account of events should the facts be challenged subsequently. It provides evidence that you took appropriate steps, which may be valuable if things go wrong later.

It is always important to be clear about who your readers are. The report may be written for a particular senior executive, but, unless it is confidential, a number of other people are likely to see it. Make sure your report is relevant to their needs too. If you are set a deadline, you will give a poor impression if you miss it. Busy managers can only cope with all the documents they receive by being selective, perhaps turning just to the introduction and summary. If they are really harassed, your report may not even leave the pending tray!

To be successful, a report must be read without undue delay, understood without undue effort, accepted and, where appropriate, acted upon. But reading a report can be a daunting experience, in which case the recipient will resist the idea of spending time wading through it. This natural resistance is known as the 'cognitive cost'. A technical, closely typed report, written in a ponderous style, without illustrations, will have a high cognitive cost. It is clearly going to be hard work absorbing the contents.

13 What point does the writer make in the first paragraph?

    A   The degree of accuracy in reports is higher now than in the past.

    B   Report writing and other forms of communication need similar skills.

    C   Readers are likely to respond favourably to attractively presented reports.

    D   The use of a computer can simplify the planning stage of a report.

14 What point is made in the second paragraph?

    A   Many people are more afraid of writing reports than they need to be.

    B   It may be difficult to decide on the appropriate length for a report.

    C   Report writing skills are influenced by the ability to speak effectively.

    D   People's careers may be affected by the way they write reports.

15 According to the third paragraph, reports are growing in importance because

    A   company size works against traditional forms of communication.

    B   shareholders demand to be kept fully informed of company activities.

    C   a greater degree of specialisation at work is becoming the norm.

    D   more people are being given responsibility for making decisions.

16 In the fourth paragraph the writer suggests that reports may be helpful if

    A   a client is dissatisfied with your advice.

    B   they are structured like the minutes of meetings.

    C   there is a disagreement about what happened.

    D   they outline a range of possible future outcomes.

17 The fifth paragraph warns that the intended reader

    A   may not agree with you about who should read your report.

    B   may not think that your report is of any value.

    C   may not accept a report that is submitted late.

    D   may not read through your report in full.

18 In the last paragraph, what is meant by 'cognitive cost'?

    A   the amount of time that the writer spends writing a report

    B   the reader's unwillingness to make an effort to understand a report

    C   the amount of time that the reader spends reading any report

    D   the writer's difficulty in presenting reports in an easily-understood style

PART FOUR

Questions 19 – 33

How to approach Reading Test Part Four
- This part of the Reading Test tests your vocabulary.
- Read the whole text quickly to find out what it is about. As you read, try to predict the words that might fill the gaps.
- Next, look at the four possible answers for each gap and cross out any obviously incorrect words.
- Then read both before and after each gap to decide which word should go in it. The word needs to fit both the meaning and the grammar.
- After completing all the gaps, read the whole text again to check your answers.

- Read the article on the opposite page about an experiment to help managers improve their work/life balance.

- Choose the best word to fill each gap from **A, B, C** or **D** below.

- For each question **19 – 33**, mark one letter (**A, B, C** or **D**) on your Answer Sheet.

- There is an example at the beginning (**0**).

Example: (Answer: B)

0	**A** defiance	**B** challenge	**C** dare	**D** confrontation
19	**A** displayed	**B** showed	**C** proved	**D** demonstrated
20	**A** control	**B** part	**C** effect	**D** place
21	**A** keep	**B** stay	**C** remain	**D** stand
22	**A** improve	**B** promote	**C** upgrade	**D** reform
23	**A** diminish	**B** reduce	**C** drop	**D** lessen
24	**A** commencing	**B** initiating	**C** originating	**D** embarking
25	**A** opening	**B** beginning	**C** outset	**D** launch
26	**A** clear out	**B** work up	**C** sort out	**D** think up
27	**A** tackle	**B** cope	**C** manage	**D** handle
28	**A** letting	**B** putting	**C** setting	**D** cutting
29	**A** Rapid	**B** Hasty	**C** Sudden	**D** Instant
30	**A** Conversely	**B** In addition	**C** Nevertheless	**D** After all
31	**A** catching	**B** running	**C** taking	**D** coming
32	**A** viewpoint	**B** attitude	**C** feeling	**D** opinion
33	**A** constant	**B** persisting	**C** stable	**D** lasting

GETTING THE BALANCE RIGHT

WORKPLACE ISSUES

Leaving work on time may not sound like much of a (**0**) ... . However, in an experiment by glass manufacturers Dartington Crystal, it (**19**) ... surprisingly difficult. Four managers, who all worked very long hours, took (**20**) ... in a simple experiment: they agreed to (**21**) ... to their set hours for a week, with no coming in early, leaving late or taking work home. The aim of the exercise was to (**22**) ... the balance between the managers' work and home lives. It was a way to get everyone thinking about their working hours and how to (**23**) ... them.

Robin Ritchie, the company's managing director, was very aware that his company was (**24**) ... on the experiment at its busiest time of the year. They were also just days away from a big product (**25**) ... . So not surprisingly, perhaps, it soon became clear that it wasn't going to be easy: even on the first day, director of design Simon Moore took home a design problem to (**26**) ... , as he couldn't relax until he had dealt with it.

As the week progressed, the four people involved found it hard to (**27**) ... with the pressure of leaving work undone. They felt they were (**28**) ... people down, and worried about the effect on the business. (**29**) ... crises made it more and more difficult to go home on time. Changing working habits wasn't easy. (**30**) ... , they saw the experiment through to the end.

There was some (**31**) ... up to do the following week, but the company did not appear to have suffered. Significantly, too, the experiment made the managers reappraise their (**32**) ... to staying late and start prioritising tasks. All in all, they felt the experiment was of (**33**) ... benefit, and that it helped them to create a better balance in their lives.

PART FIVE

Questions 34 – 45

How to approach Reading Test Part Five

- This part of the Reading Test tests your ability to identify additional or unnecessary words in a text. Most lines contain one extra word which is incorrect.
- Read the whole text quickly to find out what it is about. As you read, try to identify the words that are incorrect. Make sure you consider whole sentences, and not each line separately.
- Then read the text again, and write down the extra words.
- Remember there will be only one extra word in a line, and some lines are correct.

- Read the article on the opposite page about identifying the training needs of staff.

- In most of the lines **34 – 45** there is one extra word. It is either grammatically incorrect or does not fit in with the meaning of the text. Some lines, however, are correct.

- If a line is correct, write CORRECT on your Answer Sheet.

- If there is an extra word in the line, write the extra word in CAPITAL LETTERS on your Answer Sheet.

- The exercise begins with two examples, **(0)** and **(00)**.

Example:

0 | C | O | R | R | E | C | T | | |

00 | I | N | S | T | E | A | D | | |

Identifying training needs

0   The financial benefits of training are sometimes hard to demonstrate, and often the

00   training budget is the first to be reduced instead when spending is under pressure. For

34   this reason, and given that the need for any corporate spending to provide maximum

35   value for money, it is important for the differences between individuals must to be

36   taken into account when considering training requirements. This makes for far more

37   effective training than a programme is based solely on generalisations about staff. After

38   all this, our abilities differ, and variations in previous experience can also play a

39   significant role in learning. Identifying training needs and their capabilities on an

40   individual basis is often carried out in appraisal interviews. In those workplaces where

41   each employee's productivity is measured, such records may be considered during the

42   appraisal, allowing for the possibility that inadequate training can be identified as if the

43   reason for low productivity. Training requirements are also evaluated in such

44   assessment centres, and in which groups of staff are observed while taking part in job

45   simulation activities. Although these are often used to assess potential for promotion,
       but can also show employees' training needs within their current job.

PRACTICE TEST 2: WRITING

PART ONE

How to approach Writing Test Part One
- Part One counts for one third of the total marks in the Writing Test.
- You should spend no more than 15 minutes on Part One.
- You will be asked to write a note, memo, email or message to one or more people in your company.
- The first bullet point of the instructions outlines the situation.
- The second bullet point tells you what you should write, who you are writing it for, and the points that must be included.
- It is best to follow the order of the points that are required, as you will lose marks if you leave out any of them.

Planning
- Read the instructions carefully so that you know what to do, and underline the key words.

Writing
- Express yourself briefly and clearly.
- For a memo or email you don't need to include *to, from, date* or *subject*.
- Try to use a range of appropriate vocabulary and grammatical structures.
- Make the language suitable for the reader(s).

Checking
- After writing, read what you have written, correct mistakes and make improvements. If you want to add anything, use a sign, e.g. *. Put a line through anything you want to omit. Don't rewrite the whole of your answer.
- Make sure the examiner will be able to read your answer. Use a pen and your normal handwriting (do not write in capital letters).
- Check that you have written your answer in 40–50 words.

- You are a manager in a large retail company. The directors have recently decided to introduce a staff suggestion scheme. You have been asked to organise the introduction of the scheme.

- Write a note to your assistant:

    - saying when the scheme will begin

    - explaining the purpose of the scheme

    - asking him to inform staff about the scheme.

- Write **40 – 50** words.

NOTEPAD

To: Shaun
From: Carol

PART TWO

How to approach Writing Test Part Two

- Part Two counts for two thirds of the total marks in the Writing Test.
- You should spend about 30 minutes on Part Two.
- You will be asked to write a report, proposal or piece of business correspondence.
- You will be given information, such as a letter, advertisement, or charts and graphs, as the starting point for your answer, and will be told who to write to.
- About five 'handwritten' notes will also be given. You must use all these notes when writing your answer, and will need to invent information in connection with some of them. If you leave out any of the five notes, you will lose marks.

Planning

- Read the instructions carefully so that you know what do, and underline the key words.
- Make an outline plan, putting the five notes into a suitable order.

Writing

- Start your answer by briefly saying why you are writing.
- Express your ideas clearly.
- Try to use a wide range of appropriate vocabulary and grammatical structures.
- For a piece of business correspondence, include suitable openings and closings (e.g. *Dear Ms Smith* and *Yours sincerely* with your signature), but no addresses.
- Do not present a report or proposal in the form of a letter.
- Make the formality of the language suitable for the reader(s).

Checking

- After writing, read what you have written, correct mistakes and make improvements. If you want to add anything, use a sign, e.g. *. Put a line through anything you want to omit. Don't rewrite the whole of your answer.
- Make sure the examiner will be able to read your answer. Use a pen and your normal handwriting (do not write in capital letters).
- Check that you have written your answer in 120–140 words.

- You work for a small chain of clothing stores. The Managing Director has asked you to write a short report on last month's performance.

- Look at the charts and table below, on which you have already made some handwritten notes.

- Then, using all your handwritten notes, write the report for your Managing Director.

- Write **120 – 140** words.

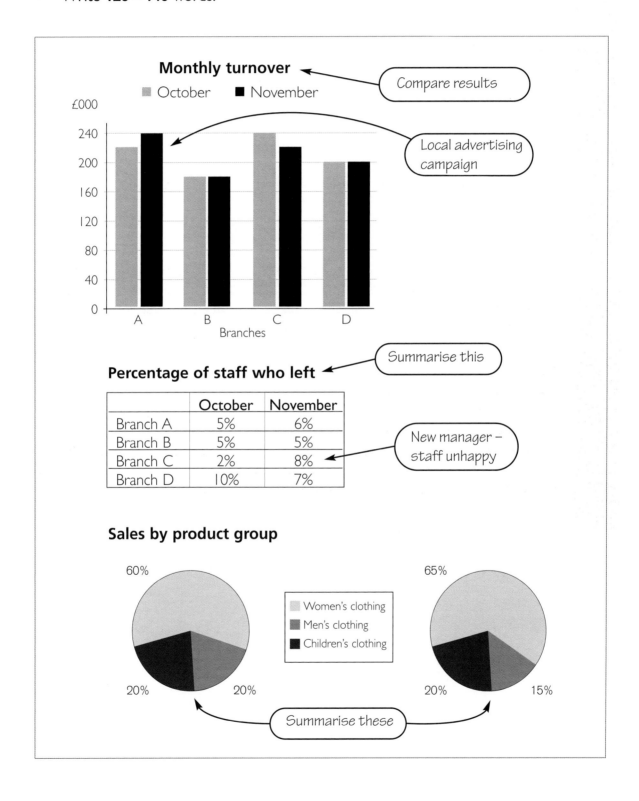

Monthly turnover

■ October ■ November

Compare results

Local advertising campaign

Percentage of staff who left

Summarise this

	October	November
Branch A	5%	6%
Branch B	5%	5%
Branch C	2%	8%
Branch D	10%	7%

New manager – staff unhappy

Sales by product group

60% 20% 20%
65% 20% 15%

■ Women's clothing
■ Men's clothing
■ Children's clothing

Summarise these

PRACTICE TEST 2: LISTENING

PART ONE
Questions 1 – 12

How to approach Listening Test Part One
- This part is in three sections. In each section you listen to a telephone conversation or message.
- You will hear each section twice before you hear the next one.
- Before you listen, read the notes. Think about what you are going to hear.
- Note all possible answers as you listen for the first time. Do not make an immediate decision.
- You should write words that you hear without changing them. They must fit the meaning of the notes.
- Decide on your final answer only after you have listened for the second time.
- Check that you have used no more than two words or a number in each numbered space.

- You will hear three telephone conversations or messages.

- Write one or two words or a number in the numbered spaces on the notes or forms.

- You will hear each recording twice.

Conversation One (Questions 1 – 4)

- Look at the notes below.

- You will hear an answerphone message about arrangements for a business trip.

Bern trip - changes

need to take (**1**) ....

have meeting with the (**2**) ....

important to check the (**3**) ....

ask to see results of (**4**) ....

Conversation Two (Questions 5 – 8)

- Look at the notes below.
- You will hear a man telephoning to ask about a recent training session.

Notes
Outcomes of training session
looking at (**5**) .... was useful
advice on (**6**) .... was valuable
the (**7**) .... was too short
next time: involve (**8**) .... in planning

Conversation Three (Questions 9 – 12)

- Look at the notes below.
- You will hear a woman telephoning about a recruitment drive.

• staff needed due to growth in (**9**) ....
• advertising to demand good (**10**) ....
• interview to include a (**11**) .... from candidates
• training programme to be designed by (**12**) ....

PART TWO

Questions 13 – 22

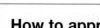

> ### How to approach Listening Test Part Two
> - This part is in two sections. In each section you listen to five short monologues, spoken by five different speakers. You will hear the first section twice, and then the second section twice.
> - For each monologue you must choose one out of eight options.
> - First read the task carefully, and make sure that you know what you need to decide.
> - Listen for the overall meaning of each monologue. Do not choose an answer just because you hear the same words in the recording as in the question.
> - Decide on your final answer only after you have listened for the second time.
> - Check that you have not used the same option more than once.

Section One (Questions 13 – 17)

- You will hear five short recordings about improvements in the workplace.

- For each recording, decide what improvement has been made.

- Write one letter (**A – H**) next to the number of the recording.

- Do not use any letter more than once.

- You will hear the five recordings twice.

13	....	**A**	Some inefficient equipment was replaced.
14	....	**B**	A bonus payment system was extended.
15	....	**C**	A department was moved to new premises.
16	....	**D**	Training opportunities were increased.
17	....	**E**	A system of cost control was implemented.
		F	Some software was upgraded.
		G	A number of specialist staff were recruited.
		H	A system of promotion was introduced.

Section Two (Questions 18 – 22)

- You will hear another five recordings.

- You will hear five speakers talking about running project teams.

- For each recording, decide what the speaker recommends.

- Write one letter (**A – H**) next to the number of the recording.

- Do not use any letter more than once.

- You will hear the five recordings twice.

18	....	**A**	Publish regular updates on progress.
		B	Provide specific training for participants.
19	....	**C**	Define individual roles clearly.
		D	Recruit members from different departments.
20	....	**E**	Check targets and deadlines frequently.
		F	Obtain input from external experts.
21	....	**G**	Examine the achievements of previous teams.
22	....	**H**	Allocate sufficient technological resources.

PART THREE

Questions 23 – 30

How to approach Listening Test Part Three
- In this part you listen twice to a long conversation, interview or monologue, and answer eight questions.
- Before you listen, read the questions. Think about what will be said.
- Note all possible answers as you listen for the first time. Do not make an immediate decision.
- Listen for overall meaning. Do not choose an answer just because you hear the same words in the recording as in the question.
- Decide on your final answer only after you have listened for the second time.

- You will hear Katherine and Andrew, students at a business school, discussing their experiences and views of business.

- For each question **23 – 30**, mark one letter (**A, B** or **C**) for the correct answer.

- You will hear the recording twice.

23 What does Katherine dislike about the course?

    A   the student presentations
    B   the reading requirements
    C   the attitude of her lecturers

24 What does she find impressive about the course?

    A   the group discussions
    B   the use of technology
    C   the focus on individuals

25 What does she think is the purpose of the latest course exercise?

    A   to improve understanding of strategy
    B   to extend knowledge of branding issues
    C   to increase ability to evaluate data

26 What aspect of the course does she find most relevant to her job?

    A   negotiating conflicting targets
    B   involving different points of view
    C   combining theory and practice

27 What does she say causes her difficulty in her job?

    A   accepting cost implications

    B   meeting tight deadlines

    C   explaining reasons for decisions

28 She hopes that in the future she will become involved with

    A   developing brand identity.

    B   negotiating strategy.

    C   improving quality control.

29 She believes that management is likely to

    A   become more creative.

    B   change its values.

    C   reduce in importance.

30 She predicts that businesses will increasingly need to respond to

    A   differences across regions.

    B   the influence of technology.

    C   changes in consumer values.

PRACTICE TEST 2: SPEAKING

PART ONE: CONVERSATION

How to approach Speaking Test Part One

- In this part of the test you answer questions about yourself and about business topics, and express opinions.
- Before the exam, think of answers to possible questions about your work or studies, business in your country, and a wide range of business-related matters. Below are some questions of the types which you might need to answer.
- In the exam, listen carefully to the questions. Make sure you answer what the examiner asks you. Ask the examiner to repeat a question if necessary. Speak to both the examiner and the other candidate, and listen to what the other candidate says.
- Try to give more than just basic answers, and give examples to show what you mean.
- Remember that you are being tested on your ability to speak in English, not on your knowledge of specific areas of business. If you do not know an answer, say so, and try to speculate.

Practise answering these questions.

> What kinds of work are most popular in your home town?
>
> Which aspect of your work/studies do you enjoy most?
>
> What are you planning to do next in your career?
>
> Do you use computers much in your work/studies?
>
> What changes in business do you expect will happen in the future?

PART TWO: INDIVIDUAL MINI-PRESENTATION

How to approach Speaking Test Part Two

- In this part of the test you give a short talk (approximately one minute) on a business topic.
- You choose one of three topics. Each one is in the form of a question beginning *What is important when … ?* There will be two words or phrases to help you develop your ideas, but it isn't essential to use these.
- You have one minute to prepare your ideas. In this time make brief notes to give you a structure and some key words.
- When you talk, make the structure clear, for example by giving a brief introduction and conclusion, and using linking words and phrases to introduce each section.
- Speak to both the examiner and the other candidate, and listen to what the other candidate says. You will have to ask the other candidate a question about their presentation after they have spoken.
- Remember that you are being tested on your ability to speak in English, not on your knowledge of specific areas of business, so if you don't know much about a topic, just say what you can about it.

Practise preparing short talks on the topics below and on the next page.

Task Sheet One

A   WHAT IS IMPORTANT WHEN…?

Making a job application

- Knowing about the company
- Preparing for questions
-
-

B   WHAT IS IMPORTANT WHEN…?

Improving customer relations

- Conducting surveys
- Regular training
-
-

C   WHAT IS IMPORTANT WHEN…?

Controlling costs

- Arrangements with suppliers
- Finance systems
-
-

Task Sheet Two

A   WHAT IS IMPORTANT WHEN...?

Introducing new technology

- Expert advice
- After-sales service
-
-

B   WHAT IS IMPORTANT WHEN...?

Dealing with clients

- Understanding needs
- Negotiating skills
-
-

C   WHAT IS IMPORTANT WHEN...?

Aiming to improve product quality

- Inspecting machinery
- Reviewing staff training
-
-

PART THREE: DISCUSSION

How to approach Speaking Test Part Three

- In this part of the test you work with the other candidate. The examiner gives you a scenario and a task to discuss. You need to have a serious discussion of the task, with the type of interaction which would be appropriate to a work environment.
- You and the other candidate should try to imagine yourselves in a work environment, faced with a real situation to discuss, on which you should try to reach some decisions.
- You have about 30 seconds to prepare your ideas. Use this time to ensure you understand the task. Ask the examiner to explain anything you are unsure of.
- Listen to the other candidate and respond to what they say. Do not just give your own opinions, or simply agree with the other candidate.
- Try to make more than just basic comments.
- Following your discussion with the other candidate, the examiner will ask you questions on the same topic. Develop your answers, and give examples to show what you mean. Listen to what the other candidate says.

Practise discussing this task and answering the questions that follow.

Promotional video

The company you work for has decided to produce a promotional video about the company and its activities.

You have been asked to make suggestions about the video.

Discuss the situation together, and decide:

- which aspects of the company should be shown in the film
- which members of staff should appear in the film.

Follow-up questions:

- Have you seen examples of effective promotional videos?
- What are the advantages to a company of having a promotional video?
- What other forms of promotion are effective?
- Might there be some forms of promotion which would not be effective?
- Do you think technology is changing the ways companies promote themselves?

Preparation

Working out the meaning: From the context

The following tips will help you find out the meaning of a word from its context:

* Work out what type of word (verb, noun, etc) fits the context.
* Look for tips, e.g. linkers such as, *that is, in addition, similarly, but, however*, which relate the unknown word to ones that you know.
* Look at the coherence of the text, e.g. is the word part of an answer to a question, or part of the solution to a problem?
* Use your knowledge to decide what is likely to be meant.

Look at this example, where *waybong* is a nonsense word:

Today this technology is the best available, but tomorrow it'll be *waybong*.

Clues to the meaning of *waybong*:

* The sentence structure makes *waybong* parallel to the phrase *the best available*. This means that *waybong* is likely to be an adjective or phrase.
* *but* shows that its meaning contrasts with *the best available*.

The phrase which *waybong* replaced is in fact *out of date*.

❶ Match *waybong* with its most likely meaning from the words in the box.

combine	revitalise	differentiate	organise
take over	evaluate	produce	speed up

1 If Farley Auto Supplies' attempt to *waybong* its rival TYK is successful, Farley's market position will be greatly strengthened.
2 Following complaints from retailers, our logistics department is to look at ways to *waybong* deliveries.
3 SK Clothing has announced that it plans to *waybong* its Magon brand with a major advertising campaign.
4 The new owners of Rackell & Smith intend to *waybong* the contribution made by each and every product line.
5 One element of Hartway Motors' plans to become more centralised is to *waybong* functions.

Grammar practice

1 For Reading Parts One and Three and all parts of the Listening test you need to understand paraphrases – different ways of expressing the same idea.

Match each sentence 1–6 with its closest paraphrase a–e. There is one extra sentence in 1–6. When you've identified it, write your own paraphrase of it, using different words as far as possible.

1 Balfour Motors is engaged in a cost-cutting programme.
2 Cogent plc is in discussions with banks about obtaining long-term loans.
3 Strong & Moore is going ahead with its strategy of diversification.
4 Beejoy Ltd is about to embark on a revamp of its outlets.
5 Walter's is on track to meet its revenue targets.
6 Jonquest anticipates a speedy recovery in its turnover.

a) This company expects that its sales income will soon rise.
b) This company still intends to broaden its range of activities.
c) This company is taking steps to reduce its expenditure.
d) This company's income is likely to be what it previously forecast.
e) This company is seeking external funding.

2 Knowing ways of carrying out various language functions is particularly useful in the Writing test. Match each sentence with the correct function from the box. There are two extra functions which you won't need to use.

accepting describing evaluating explaining predicting recommending refusing requesting action suggesting

1 The reason that we were unable to despatch your order on time was that a packaging machine malfunctioned.
2 We would be grateful if this matter could be attended to at your earliest convenience.
3 I believe that the introduction of this system would considerably improve the department's efficiency.
4 Staff turnover is likely to reach an annual rate of 25% by the end of the year.
5 You might like to discuss your future orders with one of our sales team.
6 In some respects this new printer is less suitable for our needs than the old one.
7 These two employees will be responsible for finding new business.

PRACTICE TEST 3: READING

PART ONE
Questions 1 – 7

How to approach Reading Test Part One
- In this part of the Reading Test you matchseven statements with four short texts.
- First read each short text and then read the sentences to see which ones refer to the text.
- Make sure you read each text for overall meaning. Do not choose an answer just because you can see the same words in the text.

- Look at the statements below and the views about improvement processes on the opposite page.

- Which company (**A, B, C** or **D**) does each sentence **1 – 7** refer to?

- For each sentence **1 – 7**, mark one letter (**A, B, C** or **D**) on your Answer Sheet.

- You will need to use some of the letters more than once.

Example:

0 Competition leads to efforts to achieve improvements.
(**Answer: D**)

1 Staff are invited to set the standards that are used to assess their productivity.

2 Long-term aims are negotiated with people internal and external to the company.

3 Staff contribute to the monitoring of competitors' progress.

4 Different kinds of company need to be examined for ideas for innovation.

5 Staff decide on their own requirements for training.

6 Improving one aspect of the business affects other aspects.

7 All staff are informed of the company's future direction.

A "We're ahead of our competitors in that every year we invite customers to headquarters to discuss their expectations for the next five years. In addition to customers, the meeting includes approximately 100 employees and suppliers. We parade our five-year plan, including such things as service, quality and on-time delivery, and involve everyone in a feedback process. The outcome becomes part of our long-range strategic plan, which is communicated to every employee in the organisation – a process we call management by planning."

B "The approach we find we need to take to increasing customer satisfaction is systemic. There isn't an easy way to do it. Everything is interconnected and builds. In order to delight customers, you need smooth manufacturing processes, which means you need an accurate warehouse, which in turn relies on a good manufacturing requirements system and good suppliers. You can't accomplish one in isolation."

C "As part of our improvement process, employees participate actively in raising customer satisfaction. They establish the areas in which they will be measured that translate into quality performance: things like, 'How quickly do you respond to a call?' or 'How effective are your dealings with the customer?' Feedback is provided regularly to employees. They analyse the data to determine when additional instruction and support are needed, or when processes need to be re-worked or improved, or when our goals need to be changed. They are also encouraged to keep an eye on the competition and how they are doing. These data are used for planning purposes."

D "Our senior managers are constantly pulling the competition's products apart to see what they're doing. They've also done some benchmarking against our better competitors. There are a few good ones that make us run faster and harder. But, to be honest, in terms of new service initiatives, for example, we've had to look outside our industry to find what could be called 'best of breed'. We've milked our own industry."

PART TWO

How to approach Reading Test Part Two
- In this part of the Reading Test you read a text with gaps in it, and choose the best sentence to fill each gap from a set of seven sentences.
- First read the text for the overall meaning, then go back and look for the best sentence for each gap.
- Make sure the sentence fits both the meaning and the grammar of the text around the gap.

Questions 8 – 12

- Read the article on the opposite page about the marketing guru Theodore Levitt.

- Choose the best sentence from below to fill each of the gaps.

- For each gap **8 – 12**, mark one letter (**A – G**) on your Answer Sheet.

- Do not use any letter more than once.

- There is an example at the beginning, **(0)**.

A Only a 'thoroughly customer-oriented management' can maintain it.

B It is such a far-sighted assessment that many companies are still failing it.

C They needed to reinvent their whole business by studying what customers would now want – fanbelts, say, or air cleaners.

D It is not concerned with the values that the exchange is all about.

E It set him up as the first marketing guru and over the years HBR has sold hundreds of thousands of reprints.

F These were what customers wanted after the oil price shocks of the early 1970s.

G Business in the 1950s had been a complacent, producer-oriented world.

Did this man invent marketing?

For the world of management – or the trend-setting part of it which read the Harvard Business Review (HBR) – 1960 was the year that marketing began. Extraordinary as it seems today, until HBR published an article by a German-American academic called Theodore Levitt saying that 'industry is a customer-satisfying process, not a goods-producing process', most managers operated on the principle that people would buy whatever their companies produced, with the aid of a little advertising.

(**0**) *G*. It was one where the public was so pleased to have any choice of goods after the barren years of World War II that consumer products virtually sold themselves. There might be competition between different makes of soap powder or toothpaste, but no-one in industry seriously considered probing more deeply into what customers wanted, or might want in the future.

Levitt changed all that with one article in HBR, entitled 'Marketing Myopia'. (**8**) … His message was very simple. Selling was not marketing, he pointed out. 'Selling concerns itself with the tricks and techniques of getting people to exchange their cash for your product. (**9**) … And it does not, as marketing invariably does, view the entire business process as consisting of a tightly integrated effort to discover, create, arouse and satisfy customer needs. Selling focuses on the needs of the seller, marketing on the needs of the buyer.'

Levitt began by explaining that every industry was once a growth industry. But growth will not continue through improvements in productivity or cost reduction alone. (**10**) … He cited the Detroit automobile industry as a prime example: ruled by the production ethos, in 1960 it was simply giving the customer what it thought the customer should have. 'Detroit never really researched the customer's wants. It only researched the kinds of things it had already decided to offer him,' Levitt wrote. Eventually, it was punished by the Japanese with their compact cars. (**11**) …

Industries can die if they don't understand how their markets are changing, Levitt warned, citing his famous horse-whip example: after the automobile killed the horse and carriage as personal transportation, makers of horse-whips could not save themselves by improving the product. (**12**) … These days, although Levitt called marketing a 'stepchild', it has come a long way towards growing up.

How to approach Reading Test Part Three

- In this part of the Reading Test you read a longer text and answer six questions.
- First read the questions. Try to get an idea of what the text will be about. Then read the text quickly for general understanding.
- Then read the text and questions more carefully, choosing the best answer to each question. Do not choose an answer just because you can see the same words in the text.

- Read the article below about communication and the questions on the opposite page.

- For each question **13 – 18**, mark one letter (**A**, **B**, **C** or **D**) on your Answer Sheet for the answer you choose.

How well do you communicate?

In today's fast-paced work environment, communication can come low down on your list of priorities. If you can't remember the last time you spoke to some of your friends, how do you find time to brief thousands of employees on a regular basis? That said, internal communication plays an integral part in any healthy business strategy. If done well it ensures that staff are kept abreast of the visions and values of the company they work for; if done badly it can lead to speculation and rumour.

Jenny Davenport, a director of the change management and communications consultancy, People in Business, says ongoing dialogue with staff is a necessity. 'You must educate employees to understand your business if you want them to perform,' she says. 'Unless you do, people will not trust you when times are bad.' Communication is also about discussion rather than rhetoric. Flat communication devices – email, intranets, employee publications – have a part to play but must be mixed with more interactive methods involving face-to-face contact to encourage response.

'Remember that individuals are different and like to receive information in different ways,' adds Davenport. 'As well as written communication via intranets or traditional employee magazines, team managers must talk to staff about how what they do affects the business. Twice a year, ensure employees come face to face with senior management – a conference is ideal.'

Khalid Aziz, chairman of communications consultancy The Aziz Corporation, feels that company-wide conferences are an ideal way to interact with large numbers of staff. 'It is important to organise and plan correctly,' he says. 'Have a clear aim before you start and be careful not to pack too much in – facts that can be communicated via email, for example, are a waste of conference space. Ask for response but don't ask for questions – it always sounds like a threat,' he adds. 'Get people to raise their hands if they agree with a certain statement about the company and then ask one person to elaborate.'

The intranet plays a big part in the communications strategy at One 2 One, says Neil Lovell, the company's director of communications. 'Our intranet touches everybody,' he says. 'We have set up cybercafés for staff who don't have PC access.' One 2 One's intranet carries news and general information and is supported by a monthly magazine mailed to homes, a weekly email update on matters of fact and webchats which staff are invited to join.

Getting feedback from employees is the key to hi-fi company Richer Sounds' communications policy. 'Like other businesses, we run a suggestions scheme. The difference with ours is the way it works,' says John Clayton, training and recruitment director. 'Our chairman Julian Richer reads every suggestion and we answer them all. Each proposal is rewarded with up to £25 cash – we find this is more motivational than a big prize to one employee once a year.'

13 What point is made in the first paragraph?

    A   Pressures of work have a negative effect on social relationships.

    B   Poor communication can create an atmosphere of doubt.

    C   Keeping records of employees should be a high priority.

    D   Communicating effectively can take up a lot of time.

14 According to the second paragraph, staff need to

    A   feel involved in communication processes.

    B   be supplied only with relevant information.

    C   feel that the company understands their needs.

    D   be given feedback on how well they perform.

15 Davenport suggests organising company conferences because

    A   employees will be able to meet each other.

    B   the role of team managers will be made clearer.

    C   employees will have contact with senior managers.

    D   each staff member will receive the same information.

16 What recommendation does Khalid Aziz make about holding company conferences?

    A   Encourage questions about different aspects of the company.

    B   Use email to send information related to the conference.

    C   Explain the purpose of the conference at the beginning.

    D   Invite comments on how the company is viewed.

17 Neil Lovell says that the intranet at One 2 One

    A   communicates more effectively than the magazine.

    B   is available to all members of staff.

    C   includes previously unobtainable information.

    D   is popular with all members of staff.

18 What does John Clayton say about suggestion schemes?

    A   Suggestions can be about any aspect of a company.

    B   More companies should encourage suggestions from staff.

    C   Small prizes for suggestions can be effective.

    D   Staff should be told about each other's suggestions.

PART FOUR

Questions 19 – 33

How to approach Reading Test Part Four
- This part of the Reading Test tests your vocabulary.
- Read the whole text quickly to find out what it is about. As you read, try to predict the words that might fill the gaps.
- Next, look at the four possible answers for each gap and cross out any obviously incorrect words.
- Then read both before and after each gap to decide which word should go in it. The word needs to fit both the meaning and the grammar.
- After completing all the gaps, read the whole text again to check your answers.

- Read the article on the opposite page about networking.

- Choose the best word to fill each gap from **A, B, C** or **D** below.

- For each question **19 – 33**, mark one letter (**A, B, C** or **D**) on your Answer Sheet.

- There is an example at the beginning (**0**).

Example: (Answer: A)

0	**A** old	**B** antique	**C** aged	**D** original
19	**A** measures	**B** resources	**C** means	**D** actions
20	**A** marks	**B** qualities	**C** types	**D** distinctions
21	**A** remains	**B** lasts	**C** continues	**D** keeps
22	**A** long	**B** far	**C** wide	**D** broad
23	**A** distinguished	**B** located	**C** viewed	**D** found
24	**A** ratio	**B** division	**C** proportion	**D** section
25	**A** promised	**B** assured	**C** declared	**D** warranted
26	**A** carry	**B** engage	**C** suit	**D** apply
27	**A** provide	**B** give	**C** produce	**D** offer
28	**A** induct	**B** install	**C** invest	**D** initiate
29	**A** shows	**B** proves	**C** turns	**D** results
30	**A** reference	**B** contact	**C** association	**D** connection
31	**A** trust	**B** hope	**C** expect	**D** rely
32	**A** reply	**B** reverse	**C** return	**D** respond
33	**A** orders	**B** directs	**C** insists	**D** requires

NETWORK YOUR WAY TO SUCCESS

That (**0**) ... saying, 'It's not what you know, it's who you know' sums up what may well be the most important (**19**) ... of climbing the business ladder. Diligence, competence and experience are fine (**20**) ..., but they are not enough.

While this is no great secret, the fact (**21**) ... that skilled workers are few and (**22**) ... between – yet business success depends on informal networking and sociologists have (**23**) ... that the majority of top jobs in the US are obtained through it. A vast (**24**) ... of jobs are never advertised and of those that are, many have already been (**25**) ... to someone known to the company. These processes (**26**) ... not just to industry but to the government and public sector as well.

Potentially, colleagues, superiors, business friends, customers, suppliers can (**27**) ... a networker with information, addresses and open doors that make the difference between stagnation and a rapid rise. Nonetheless, as a communications trainer in Germany put it: 'Many people just do not know how to (**28**) ..., develop and foster promising relationships.' For some, networking (**29**) ... just too time-consuming or stressful. Such individuals shut themselves in their office and minimise (**30**) ... with the outside world. They may do a great job of work, but they are unlikely to make great career strides. Other would-be networkers (**31**) ... instant results, make a real nuisance of themselves, or network in too limited an environment. There are plenty of other classic errors, ranging from a failure to (**32**) ... favours, to the converse – networking with opportunists who themselves never deliver.

Effective networking does not just happen. It is a conscious process of developing links which (**33**) ... creativity, energy and commitment. Learning to do it will pay dividends.

PART FIVE

Questions 34 – 45

How to approach Reading Test Part Five

- This part of the Reading Test tests your ability to identify additional or unnecessary words in a text. Most lines contain one extra word which is incorrect.
- Read the whole text quickly to find out what it is about. As you read, try to identify the words that are incorrect. Make sure you consider whole sentences, and not each line separately.
- Then read the text again, and write down the extra words.
- Remember there will be only one extra word in a line, and some lines are correct.

- Read the text on the opposite page about running meetings.

- In most of the lines **34 – 45** there is one extra word. It is either grammatically incorrect or does not fit in with the meaning of the text. Some lines, however, are correct.

- If a line is correct, write CORRECT on your Answer Sheet.

- If there is an extra word in the line, write the extra word in CAPITAL LETTERS on your Answer Sheet.

- The exercise begins with two examples, (**0**) and (**00**).

Example:

0 | C | O | R | R | E | C | T | | | |

00 | O | N | | | | | | | | |

MAKE SURE YOUR MEETINGS RUN SMOOTHLY

0   A well run meeting can achieve much, but a badly run meeting is unlikely

00   to achieve anything, and indeed may damage on an important project's

34   progress. Meetings should create a sense of the harmony, but they can

35   cause confusion. In normal circumstances, so meetings should be planned

36   well in advance, both in terms of who will attend it and what will be discussed.

37   Overcrowded meetings suggest managers lack their self-confidence and

38   mean there will be too much of discussion on every minor point. The only

39   points that should be discussed are those that require a decision. If you need

40   your staff to update you on something, ask them to send information you

41   can read in your own time. Before a meeting starts, establish for the finishing

42   time, and stick to it. If you let one only meeting run over, then all your meetings

43   will. Make sure the purpose of the meeting is clear there to all concerned, so

44   that everyone stays as focused. Coffee breaks should be regular, and taken

45   away from the table, to maintain energy and concentration at optimum levels.

PRACTICE TEST 3: WRITING

PART ONE

How to approach Writing Test Part One
- Part One counts for one third of the total marks in the Writing Test.
- You should spend no more than 15 minutes on Part One.
- You will be asked to write a note, memo, email or message to one or more people in your company.
- The first bullet point of the instructions outlines the situation.
- The second bullet point tells you what you should write, who you are writing it for, and the points that must be included.
- It is best to follow the order of the points that are required, as you will lose marks if you leave out any of them.

Planning
- Read the instructions carefully so that you know what to do, and underline the key words.

Writing
- Express yourself briefly and clearly.
- For a memo or email you don't need to include *to, from, date* or *subject*.
- Try to use a range of appropriate vocabulary and grammatical structures.
- Make the language suitable for the reader(s).

Checking
- After writing, read what you have written, correct mistakes and make improvements. If you want to add anything, use a sign, e.g. *. Put a line through anything you want to omit. Don't rewrite the whole of your answer.
- Make sure the examiner will be able to read your answer. Use a pen and your normal handwriting (do not write in capital letters).
- Check that you have written your answer in 40–50 words.

- You are the manager of the marketing department in your company. A new assistant manager has recently been appointed and will start work soon.

- Write an email to all staff in the department:

  - explaining the need for the appointment

  - saying when the assistant manager will start work

  - describing the experience the assistant manager has.

- Write **40 – 50** words.

New assistant manager

From: Candace Woodward
To: All marketing staff
Subject: **New assistant manager**

PART TWO

How to approach Writing Test Part Two

- Part Two counts for two thirds of the total marks in the Writing Test.
- You should spend about 30 minutes on Part Two.
- You will be asked to write a report, proposal or piece of business correspondence.
- You will be given information, such as a letter, advertisement, or charts and graphs, as the starting point for your answer, and will be told who to write to.
- About five 'handwritten' notes will also be given. You must use all these notes when writing your answer, and will need to invent information in connection with some of them. If you leave out any of the five notes, you will lose marks.

Planning

- Read the instructions carefully so that you know what do, and underline the key words.
- Make an outline plan, putting the five notes into a suitable order.

Writing

- Start your answer by briefly saying why you are writing.
- Express your ideas clearly.
- Try to use a wide range of appropriate vocabulary and grammatical structures.
- For a piece of business correspondence, include suitable openings and closings (e.g. *Dear Ms Smith* and *Yours sincerely* with your signature), but no addresses.
- Do not present a report or proposal in the form of a letter.
- Make the formality of the language suitable for the reader(s).

Checking

- After writing, read what you have written, correct mistakes and make improvements. If you want to add anything, use a sign, e.g. *. Put a line through anything you want to omit. Don't rewrite the whole of your answer.
- Make sure the examiner will be able to read your answer. Use a pen and your normal handwriting (do not write in capital letters).
- Check that you have written your answer in 120–140 words.

- You work for Jango, a kitchen furniture manufacturer. Jango wants to start selling in Scotland, and is looking for an agency to handle its advertising there. In a business directory you have seen an entry for the advertising agency Westgate & Steyne.

- Read Westgate & Steyne's entry below, on which you have made some notes.

- Then, using all your notes, write a letter to Marion Westgate at Westgate & Steyne.

- Write **120 – 140** words.

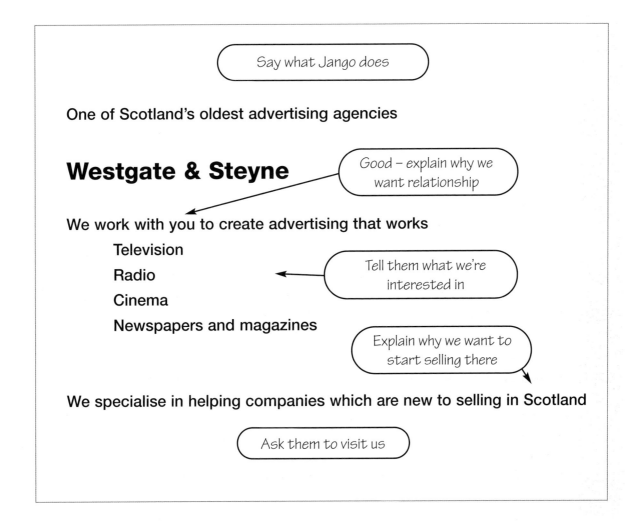

PRACTICE TEST 3: LISTENING

PART ONE
Questions 1 – 12

> ### How to approach Listening Test Part One
> - This part is in three sections. In each section you listen to a telephone conversation or message.
> - You will hear each section twice before you hear the next one.
> - Before you listen, read the notes. Think about what you are going to hear.
> - Note all possible answers as you listen for the first time. Do not make an immediate decision.
> - You should write words that you hear without changing them. They must fit the meaning of the notes.
> - Decide on your final answer only after you have listened for the second time.
> - Check that you have used no more than two words or a number in each numbered space.

- You will hear three telephone conversations or messages.

- Write one or two words or a number in the numbered spaces on the notes or forms.

- You will hear each recording twice.

Conversation One (Questions 1 – 4)

- Look at the notes below.

- You will hear a man telephoning his office from a trade fair.

Message from John – trade fair

• new (**1**) .... is very popular

• most orders taken for (**2**) .... package

• not many orders for (**3**) .... software

• send more (**4**) .... today

Conversation Two (Questions 5 – 8)

• Look at the notes below.

• You will hear a woman leaving a message about a meeting.

TODAY BUSINESS MAGAZINE

Message

To: Stephanie   **From**: Celia

At Monday's meeting:

• report results of latest (**5**) ....

• discuss new (**6**) .... section

• agree changes in (**7**) ....

NB: circulate examples of (**8**) .... before meeting

Conversation Three (Questions 9 – 12)

• Look at the notes below.

• You will hear a woman telephoning about a recent report.

Report – summary

programme of (**9**) .... is effective

introduction of (**10**) .... was worthwhile

current (**11**) .... lacks focus

Important: review results with the (**12**) ....

next week

PART TWO

Questions 13 – 22

How to approach Listening Test Part Two
- This part is in two sections. In each section you listen to five short monologues, spoken by five different speakers. You will hear the first section twice, and then the second section twice.
- For each monologue you must choose one out of eight options.
- First read the task carefully, and make sure that you know what you need to decide.
- Listen for the overall meaning of each monologue. Do not choose an answer just because you hear the same words in the recording as in the question.
- Decide on your final answer only after you have listened for the second time.
- Check that you have not used the same option more than once.

Section One (Questions 13 – 17)

- You will hear five speakers talking about their work.
- For each recording, decide what the speaker is trying to achieve.
- Write one letter (**A – H**) next to the number of the recording.
- Do not use any letter more than once.
- You will hear the five recordings twice.

13	**A**	to speed up project completion times
	B	to cut expenditure on temporary staff
14	**C**	to rationalise the system of record-keeping
15	**D**	to combine functions across departments
	E	to save time spent in meetings
16	**F**	to co-ordinate projects on different sites
	G	to streamline the recruitment process
17	**H**	to reduce differences among targets

Section Two (Questions 18 – 22)

- You will hear five speakers talking about business trips.

- For each recording, choose the reason the speaker gives for the trip.

- Write one letter (**A – H**) next to the number of the recording.

- Do not use any letter more than once.

- You will hear the five recordings twice.

18	....	

A   to re-negotiate a contract

B   to inspect the condition of some equipment

19 ....

C   to meet a potential client

D   to attend a strategy planning meeting

20 ....

E   to visit a trade fair

21 ....

F   to recruit a new agent

G   to investigate potential premises

22 ....

H   to review the results of a survey

PART THREE
Questions 23 – 30

How to approach Listening Test Part Three
- In this part you listen twice to a long conversation, interview or monologue, and answer eight questions.
- Before you listen, read the questions. Think about what will be said.
- Note all possible answers as you listen for the first time. Do not make an immediate decision.
- Listen for overall meaning. Do not choose an answer just because you hear the same words in the recording as in the question.
- Decide on your final answer only after you have listened for the second time.

- You will hear two managers, Louis and Sally, discussing changes in their company.

- For each question **23 – 30**, mark one letter (**A**, **B** or **C**) for the correct answer.

- You will hear the recording twice.

23 Sally says that the changes were planned by

        A   a cross-departmental team.

        B   management consultants.

        C   the company chairman.

24 She says the changes are designed to deal with

        A   high staff turnover.

        B   increased costs.

        C   falling sales.

25 What does Louis feel about the changes?

        A   They should have happened sooner.

        B   Some managers will dislike them.

        C   Their success will be limited.

26 Sally says the new working hours will be

        A   less productive in the long run.

        B   unpopular with some staff.

        C   difficult to control.

27 She thinks that the new sales targets

    A   fail to consider competitors.

    B   are too high for her department.

    C   should vary according to the product.

28 Louis thinks the new training will be effective because

    A   it is available on-line.

    B   it covers more topics.

    C   it uses outside trainers.

29 Sally says that the newsletter will be most valuable for

    A   new staff.

    B   management.

    C   agents abroad.

30 What does she think will happen in six months' time?

    A   There will be new policies.

    B   Staff morale will be higher.

    C   Consultants will be hired.

PRACTICE TEST 3: SPEAKING

PART ONE: CONVERSATION

How to approach Speaking Test Part One
- In this part of the test you answer questions about yourself and about business topics, and express opinions.
- Before the exam, think of answers to possible questions about your work or studies, business in your country, and a wide range of business-related matters. Below are some questions of the types which you might need to answer.
- In the exam, listen carefully to the questions. Make sure you answer what the examiner asks you. Ask the examiner to repeat a question if necessary. Speak to both the examiner and the other candidate, and listen to what the other candidate says.
- Try to give more than just basic answers, and give examples to show what you mean.
- Remember that you are being tested on your ability to speak in English, not on your knowledge of specific areas of business. If you do not know an answer, say so, and try to speculate.

Practise answering these questions.

What kind of job would you most like to have?

What are the main products made in your home town?

How important do you think suitable packaging is for products?

What attracts you to buy particular products?

What types of business in general do you think will be most successful in the future?

PART TWO: INDIVIDUAL MINI-PRESENTATION

How to approach Speaking Test Part Two
- In this part of the test you give a short talk (approximately one minute) on a business topic.
- You choose one of three topics. Each one is in the form of a question beginning *What is important when … ?* There will be two words or phrases to help you develop your ideas, but it isn't essential to use these.
- You have 1 minute to prepare your ideas. In this time make brief notes to give you a structure and some key words.
- When you talk, make the structure clear, for example by giving a brief introduction and conclusion, and using linking words and phrases to introduce each section.
- Speak to both the examiner and the other candidate, and listen to what the other candidate says. You will have to ask the other candidate a question about their presentation after they have spoken.
- Remember that you are being tested on your ability to speak in English, not on your knowledge of specific areas of business, so if you don't know much about a topic, just say what you can about it.

Practise preparing short talks on the topics below and on the next page.

Task Sheet One

A   WHAT IS IMPORTANT WHEN…?

Advertising a product or service

- Appropriate media
- Competition
-
-

B   WHAT IS IMPORTANT WHEN…?

Preparing to attend a conference

- Information about the speakers
- Planning the journey
-
-

C   WHAT IS IMPORTANT WHEN…?

Setting targets

- Staff morale
- Planning
-
-

Task Sheet Two

A   WHAT IS IMPORTANT WHEN...?

Managing staff

- Motivation
- Experience
-
-

B   WHAT IS IMPORTANT WHEN...?

Attracting investment

- Strategic planning
- Public relations
-
-

C   WHAT IS IMPORTANT WHEN...?

Preparing for a product launch

- People involved
- Costs
-
-

PART THREE: DISCUSSION

How to approach Speaking Test Part Three
- In this part of the test you work with the other candidate. The examiner gives you a scenario and a task to discuss. You need to have a serious discussion of the task, with the type of interaction which would be appropriate to a work environment.
- You and the other candidate should try to imagine yourselves in a work environment, faced with a real situation to discuss, on which you should try to reach some decisions.
- You have about 30 seconds to prepare your ideas. Use this time to ensure you understand the task. Ask the examiner to explain anything you are unsure of.
- Listen to the other candidate and respond to what they say. Do not just give your own opinions, or simply agree with the other candidate.
- Try to make more than just basic comments.
- Following your discussion with the other candidate, the examiner will ask you questions on the same topic. Develop your answers, and give examples to show what you mean. Listen to what the other candidate says.

Practise discussing this task and answering the questions that follow.

Relocation

The company you work for is considering re-locating to larger premises outside the city centre.

You have been asked to make recommendations concerning this possibility.

Discuss the situation together, and decide:

- what advantages there could be in re-locating
- what difficulties the re-location might cause.

Follow-up questions:

- Have you worked in different locations?
- Where would you most like to work?
- What disadvantages are there to city centre locations?
- What effects does technology have on the design of premises nowadays?
- Do you think globalisation is changing the way companies do business?

TAPESCRIPTS

Practice Test 1

Part One (CD Tracks 01–04)

Section One (CD Track 02)

M Business faculty office.

F Hello, my name's Sylvia Carlyle. I've had a letter accepting me on a course, and asking me to phone about the optional modules.

M Let me find your details. OK, you're taking marketing fundamentals, aren't you?

F Actually I applied for marketing originally, then changed to personnel practice, and that's in the acceptance letter.

M The database hasn't been updated. No problem. Right, have you chosen your two modules?

F I'm interested in health and safety.

M You have to do that anyway, as part of the course.

F Oh, then I'm confused about what's optional and what's compulsory. What about pay systems?

M Yes, that's optional.

F OK. I'll do that as my first module.

M And for module B?

F Is decision making possible?

M Yes. Now what about your term paper?

F I'm thinking of calling it 'Assumptions and behaviour within companies'.

M We just need the general field at this stage. Shall I enter that as organisational culture?

F Fine.

M OK, Sylvia, we'll look forward to seeing you at the beginning of term. Goodbye.

F Goodbye.

Section Two (CD Track 03)

You're through to the Sandridge Centre vacancies hotline. We are an online publisher providing essential business information for governments, trade organisations and investors. We are currently looking for an industrial analyst to join our expanding staff of experts, whose role is to assess the investment climate and provide high-quality information about industries around the world.

The person appointed will join specialists in pensions and banking in our financial services team. As he or she will concentrate on insurance, considerable knowledge of this field is essential. Other industries that we cover include telecoms and healthcare.

As our staff need to collect and analyse a great deal of data, only applicants with research experience will be considered. Shortlisted candidates will be asked to provide evidence of this.

Preference will be given to candidates with regional expertise. This could be derived from study or from working abroad. Applications, consisting of a CV and covering letter, should be sent to the Human Resources Manager before the end of this month. Thank you for phoning.

Section Three (CD Track 04)

F Workstations department.

M Hello. I'm calling from Crawford's, the accountants. We're looking for something to stand a computer on.

F Right. Are you interested in a PC table, which is designed to hold a computer, monitor and keyboard, and still give plenty of working space, or a more compact terminal table, without the working space?

M Oh, the smaller one will do. It's for a computer that we don't use much.

F OK. Well, we have two versions: there's height adjustable and standard.

M The first, I think, as different people will be using it.

F And are you interested in a mouse shelf or side extensions, both of which come extra?

M I don't think so. Oh, perhaps a mouse shelf. Will it fit on either side of the keyboard?

F Yes.

M Is there anywhere to put a printer?

F Well there's nothing integral, but you can buy a printer stand, which is separate and fits underneath the table.

M OK, I'll probably do that. I'll come in and have a look at the equipment.

F Fine. We're open until …

Part Two (CD Tracks 05–08)

Section One (CD Track 06)

13 My job involves making sure the firm's accounting systems run as efficiently as possible. There are always new problems to solve, so there's a bit of a challenge. But I've been there long enough, and I'm ready for a change. I'm planning to go freelance, and offer the same sort of service to a variety of companies. I'm sure I've gained enough knowledge over the years, and I'd like to be able to tackle a greater range of problems.

14 The company I work for has a new system of

working with overseas partners, and people are encouraged to move abroad for a year or two. It's a chance to learn different ways of working, of course. I would be prepared to do it if I could be sure it was a stepping stone to becoming head of department, instead of just finance administrator as I am now. Though if I could achieve that without relocating, I'd prefer it.

15 I'm in a very specialised area of technology, and actually the future's all mapped out for me, because I can continue up the ladder until I'm in charge of the section. But I've had enough, and my ambition now is to get right away from it and try something new. I don't think that the company I'm in now would let me change jobs internally, so I'll probably have to move to another firm, or set up on my own.

16 Honestly, my firm won't stay in business much longer, it's so inefficient. Take the sales staff – they waste time on the road because they each deal with different customers in the same area. I would change that. I've got plenty of ideas for improvements, but there's no system for putting them forward. It'd be easier if I was more senior, but I enjoy my present work. I'd just like to see my ideas being implemented. Then the job would be perfect.

17 I work for quite a small advertising agency, and we set up a team for each new project. My job covers both design and responsibility for leading project teams, currently one on a major advertising campaign. I was totally new to project management when I joined the company, but now I find it fascinating. I'm planning to talk to my line manager about altering the balance and doing more of that. Then the job would be ideal.

Section Two (CD Track 08)

18 I used to work for an employment agency which supplied staff to civil engineering companies. We were growing fast, opening branches in more countries every year. Well, that was great. But instead of investing properly to get a good location for each branch, the company preferred to rent cheap premises and to pour resources into the head office, which of course very few of the customers ever saw. It made most of the staff in the branches very unhappy.

19 I've always loved racing cars, so a couple of friends and I started our own small business manufacturing them. But I had no idea how difficult it was going to be! You see there's been a lot of innovation in racing cars since I was a child. Nowadays they're full of electronic

components, which we sourced from specialist firms. But we could never be sure of getting them on time, so of course that caused lots of delays in production.

20 Certain things must be right, from the outset. Take staff: employing people you can't depend on is very harmful. And when you're trying to break into a market with goods identical to your competitors' products, you need to undercut them. But my last company did the opposite when they targeted a new region, and expected consumers to pay twenty per cent more. Obviously you can only sell at a premium if you're selling something new, or offering added value.

21 Customers are much less loyal these days, so companies have to work hard to get repeat sales. And that means having staff who really understand customer care, and identifying what will sell. But of course demand changes. My first job was with an electronics firm that just didn't keep up with technical developments. They assumed there would always be a demand for their goods, and let their competitors get ahead of them. As a result, they went out of business.

22 Some years ago I set up a small company to produce high quality food. I found organic farmers to supply all the ingredients, and used traditional recipes from around the world. We were producing small quantities so it was hard to keep prices competitive, but we managed it. My decision to sell through small, independent food stores was a mistake, though, because many of them were losing customers to the supermarkets, so sales were much lower than I expected.

Part Three (CD Tracks 09–10)

Today's case study concerns a merger between two supermarket chains, and subsequent problems. Before I hand out the documentation, here's a quick overview.

Five years ago, Kelway Supermarkets merged with its low-cost rival Duncan, to form a company called KD. Although the new business was still far smaller than the chief players in the retail food sector, analysts believed its increased size would allow KD to put pressure on its suppliers to keep their prices down. However, Duncan and Kelway both had strong, rather different images, and doubts were expressed about how well they fitted together.

The merger wasn't successful. The company maintained both chains, while converting some of the low-cost Duncan stores to the Kelway format, which meant these rebranded stores took on Kelway's name, product range and higher prices. The conversion was possible once the supply chains of the two brands had been unified. But this policy seriously underestimated the difference between the customers of the two chains, and the rebranded stores lost customers. However, fears of competition from foreign supermarkets moving into the country failed to materialise.

Another problem resulted from the new structure introduced after the merger. With two sets of senior managers competing for positions, there was a risk of allocating them equally to the two chains, rather than on merit. The negotiations led to a satisfactory outcome, however, which included Kelway's former chief executive becoming responsible for stores, and Duncan's taking charge of systems, supply chain and logistics. Both worked conscientiously for the good of both chains. However, certain problems slipped between the two of them and failed to be resolved.

After two years of poor results, increasing KD's debt burden, the company decided to sell off a number of stores, particularly on out-of-town sites, which were too large to fit its new concept. The sale was intended to fund the transformation of both chains into convenience retailers, operating particularly in town centres, on petrol forecourts and within department stores. Unfortunately, though, few companies were interested in purchasing the sites which were for sale.

KD believes its appeal to customers is the fact that it's a discounter, and hopes that the resulting high sales volume will compensate for its thin profit margins. This is a strong feature of its advertising, which even makes direct comparisons with its competitors, and the company has never felt the need to follow other supermarkets in setting up loyalty schemes to encourage repeat custom.

Despite its efforts, though, sales are still falling. Last month the Chairman admitted that this wasn't caused by the general market slowdown, as KD is underperforming most other supermarket chains. While rejecting claims that the company is still suffering from internal stresses, he acknowledged the chief cause by launching a change of philosophy: for the first time the company will find out what purchasers actually want in its supermarkets.

The Chairman also announced several further moves to turn round the company's performance. One is to examine new ways of promoting the brands, in order to spend the advertising budget as effectively as possible. Secondly, the company will take a close look at all its suppliers, to ensure that they are the best ones to use. And thirdly, the range of goods on offer will be significantly broadened, to attract a wider spectrum of customers.

OK, that briefly is the recent history of KD. Your first task is to identify all the factors which have contributed to the company's troubles since the merger, and assess how it dealt with each of them. Take the merger itself as given. After that we'll look at where the company goes from here. So could you pass round these papers, and then start work.

Practice Test 2

Part One (CD Tracks 11–14)

Section One (CD Track 12)

Dave. Hi, this is Helen. Sorry this is late notice, but I just need to update you on the trip to Bern – there've been some changes. First, something for your briefcase. We're holding prices on the list at the same level as last year, but with all the product changes, you do need to have the latest catalogue with you. And, on top of talking to the marketing people, you'll need to set up a meeting with someone – I've just found out they've appointed a new IT co-ordinator, so you'll need to organise a session with him, obviously. And it's vital that you set aside some time to go through the strategy document carefully – it's got to be agreed soon, before we set the new targets. And finally – sorry there's so much! – they've been carrying out some market research, so be sure, once you've done your presentation, you remember to say you want to see the findings – should be interesting. OK, well that's it for the time being.

Section Two (CD Track 13)

F   Amanda Sharpe.

M   Oh hi, Mandy. I just wanted to ask how the training day went. I'm sorry I couldn't be there.

F   Hi, Jim. Yes, we missed you. Well, it was good overall. There was a rather familiar presentation of theory, and then some very informative case studies to discuss. We also spent time reviewing important staffing issues, and there were some tips given on teamwork that we can definitely put into practice.

M   Sounds excellent.

F Yes, although the afternoon session seemed to go on and on. I found it hard to concentrate, but when I looked at the handout afterwards for the main points, it was very brief, and didn't say much. Anyway, there's another one next month. I've suggested the training manager consults with the HR supervisor in setting it up, to make sure it's all relevant. I hope you'll be able to make it.

M Yes, I'll be free for that one.

Section Three (CD Track 14)

M Carol, hello – I gather you wanted to speak to me.

F Oh yes, George, thanks for calling. It's about the recruitment we need to do.

M OK.

F There'll be a lot more to do with the new contract, meaning export sales are going to rise, but we've got to make sure we attract the right kind of people. So when you draw up the copy for the advertisement, will you put in something about their needing to be strong in communication skills rather than just languages, which don't necessarily guarantee what we want?

M Sure.

F And I think we'll need to make the interviews effective. We ought to test them in some way, and getting them to give a presentation – nothing very complicated – will achieve that, I think. Now, once they've been selected, it'll be down to the quality of the training they get. Rather than overloading Personnel, I've asked the Sales Director to put together a programme.

M That makes sense. I'll get started on the ad.

Part Two (CD Tracks 15–18)

Section One (CD Track 16)

13 Growth for a new business like ours can be as much of a problem as a positive. You're struggling to keep up on all fronts, and the people side of things can be a real headache. What we do is rather specialised, which means you can't just take people on as and when you need them. That's why making the skills building sessions available to more people was a good idea, as it means we can grow expertise internally.

14 Well, it is a step in the right direction, although there's still a long way to go before we can really maximise our potential. But using the database had been difficult, because we were running it on such old PCs and they kept crashing. Now we've got high quality ones, it should all start to go more smoothly. Though of course training to work with them is still an issue.

15 Small businesses can be incredibly inefficient in all sorts of ways. We've certainly been guilty of paying out for things without checking the outlay against the benefits. But with this new chap appointed, I can see we're going to be much more careful. We have to put everything to him, and he analyses all spending. Waste is going right down, and we've cancelled some orders for unnecessary new machinery. Margins are looking better already.

16 If we want to stick to our plan for growth, then we have to make sure that we retain staff. We certainly can't afford to keep taking on new people and training them up. I think we were right to drop the purely financial rewards for meeting targets – people are as interested in long-term security as in cash. But the prospect of moving up to the new team leader level seems to be a stronger incentive – a good decision.

17 It was very complicated to arrange, but now we're seeing the benefits. There just wasn't enough room for everyone and everything. People had to keep going downstairs to do copying, and they could hear each other's phone calls – very distracting. But setting admin up in the new building has given everyone room to breathe, and the atmosphere in both places is better now. The next thing will be upgrading the PCs.

Section Two (CD Track 18)

18 Well, obviously every team's going to be different, but some things should be standard practice. For the thing to hold together, everyone's got to be pulling their weight, whatever their role is, so you need to keep a keen eye on how they're all doing. Keep tabs on whether they've done what they should have, and whether they're getting things done on time. You need to be equal and fair with everyone.

19 If you're putting people together for a particular purpose on top of their normal work, you need to be sure they've got everything they need to fulfil their brief. Communication is a key factor, so be sure they have the tools to achieve quality on that front – a laptop for meetings, a bulletin board on the intranet and so on. Special teams need high visibility to keep their motivation up, and to maintain interest among other staff.

20 There's no point re-inventing the wheel for every team. You can look outside the current group for ideas. See what teams in other departments or divisions have managed to do – you'll often find they've worked in similar circumstances, and you can look at how they handled it. That'll give you ideas of what to do – and, often, what not to do, too. It should mean your own progress is smoother.

21 The trouble is that when things seem to go wrong, it may be too late to fix them, because you actually built the problem in from the start. It's vital that each member of the team knows exactly what it is he or she is supposed to contribute. You won't get a good whole if the parts aren't put together properly. If members are from different departments, they'll have different expectations, which need to be dealt with.

22 A team can look like a single unit from the outside, but be chaos within, with nobody really understanding what's going on. Or, as often happens, they have conflicting ideas of what they're trying to achieve. It can help to avoid such problems if you build in an education phase at the start – make sure everyone is fully inducted by teaching them the skills they'll need for the project. It'll make life easier – or bearable, at least.

Part Three (CD Tracks 19–20)

M   Well, Katherine, I've only been on the course for a few weeks, but you're in your third and final year.

F   Yes, there's light at the end of the tunnel. It's hard, doing it part-time.

M   Have you enjoyed it?

F   Oh, on balance, yes, very much. It's not perfect, of course. The teaching staff vary in their commitment, but I think I've been lucky in getting the more dynamic ones. And most of the students are fine – there are a few oddballs – and there's such a mix of backgrounds and expertise, which comes out in the really wide range of presentations we get. One down side is the number of books and journals we're expected to get through – some weeks it's just been too much.

M   Yes, I'm finding that already. What have you particularly enjoyed?

F   One thing that's struck me is how much each person is capable of contributing. We have these online chat rooms and email lists, so you can stay in touch with each other, but nobody says anything special. And then when we have the class sessions, suddenly everyone comes to life, and you get some great exchanges of ideas.

M   Interesting. And what are you working on at the moment?

F   We've got a tough assignment. They've given us a case study about a company's plans to re-brand, and we have to go through all the figures – sales, research et cetera – and comment on them. It's supposed to give us practice in drawing conclusions from the figures available. But it's hard!

M   I know I'm not ready for that kind of thing yet. But do you find the course relevant to your work?

F   Most of it, yes. It's been very helpful in showing me how to bring together attitudes and contributions from different parts of my company – bringing in the aims of both the marketing and the finance departments, for example, in order to generate new ideas. That's been of real practical value for me at work.

M   So it's made your job easier?

F   Oh, I wouldn't go that far! I've got a demanding role, and whatever the project we're involved in, everything's always got to be done yesterday, so there's the constant stress of working in a hurry. It means doing costings, setting targets, and so on, at the same time, along with providing a detailed rationale for everything you've decided on.

M   Sounds extremely demanding. But do you find it rewarding? Will you stay there?

F   It's fine for now. What I'm hoping to do is arrange a shift in direction, to get a more strategic role, perhaps next year, when the course is out of the way. The company's working on quality control at the moment, which isn't hugely interesting for me, but the next major project is on building up our brand image, and I'd like to play an active part in that.

M   So you look forward to a long career in management?

F   Oh, yes – it's exciting, because it's changing all the time. And as many companies downsize, or focus on core activities through outsourcing, it becomes more key. It will continue to find ever more inventive solutions, new ways to apply its values.

M   Yes, but business is bound to change, isn't it?

F   For sure. Globalisation's being assisted by

developments in technology, meaning that companies are getting used to catering for far more regional and national markets, but at the same time customers are starting to shift in what they want to see. They're expressing their concern about the environment, for example, and companies will have to take that into account.

M *I'm sure you're right. Well, shall we ...*

Practice Test 3

Part One (CD Tracks 21–24)

Section One (CD Track 22)

John here. I'm calling from the fair. Things are going pretty well. I thought you'd like an update. OK, well, you'll be pleased to know that the high resolution monitor looks good on the stand, and we're getting a very warm reception for the latest scanner, which is encouraging. The stand's fairly crowded most of the time. In terms of actual sales, it's the wireless cable set that's performing best. The new keyboard's also doing OK, so there's plenty of good news. I have to say that I'm a bit disappointed with the take-up for the automatic typing software, as I thought that would sell really well. Perhaps it'll pick up in time. We'll need to give it some thought. What else? Oh, yes – the e-cards are great. That was an inspired idea. Everyone's taking a copy of the brochure, so I'm glad we brought the extra boxes. And we're getting through the demonstration disks quickly – can you get some more sent down this afternoon? I think that's everything. Bye.

Section Two (CD Track 23)

M *Stephanie Mallet's phone.*

F *Is Stephanie there?*

M *I'm afraid she's out all day. Can I take a message?*

F *Would you? It's Celia. She'll need to know a couple of things in advance of Monday's meeting. There's a lot to get through on the day. After we've gone through the sales figures, we'll have her outline what we can learn from the reader survey conducted last month. But she'll have to keep it brief. Then we'll be wanting her to contribute ideas for the e-commerce pages – should we model that on the IT supplement, or do something different? In fact, we need to make a decision on the alterations to the lay-out during the meeting.*

We can't put it off any longer.

M *Right, I think I've got all that. Anything else?*

F *Oh yes, I need her to print off the cover designs and send them round, so we can all think about them before the meeting. It'll save a bit of time. Thanks.*

M *Thank you.*

Section Three (CD Track 24)

M *Hello.*

F *Fred. Hi, I thought I should let you know about the consultant's report. It won't be printed up until next week, but I can tell you the main points.*

M *Oh good, yes. Fire away.*

F *Well, it's a mixed bag, really. Bringing in outside trainers remains a possibility, but in the meantime the series of in-house training sessions is described as working well and producing good results.*

M *That's good to hear.*

F *And also on the plus side he said that starting up the suggestion scheme was useful, and went on to endorse the proposal for the intranet, so we seem to be getting some things right.*

M *What a relief.*

F *However ...*

M *Oh dear!*

F *He is worried about staffing issues, and criticises our present recruitment, which he says needs to be better directed. He doesn't think we're attracting the right people.*

M *We'll need to work on that.*

F *Anyway, we'll discuss all the findings next week. The MD's asked the development group to get together for that.*

M *I'll see you then.*

Part Two (CD Tracks 25–28)

Section One (CD Track 26)

13 *It's a cliché, isn't it: 'our biggest asset is our people'? But if it's true, we're in real trouble here. Staff turnover's alarmingly high, with far too many people going off to talk to recruitment agencies. It's the same across the board, in every department. And it's costing a fortune in paying short-term people to fill the gaps. I want to increase levels of satisfaction in order to increase retention and stop wasting money.*

14 *It ought to be a fairly straightforward management task, so I don't know why it's proving so difficult. Of course we need to get together to review progress at each stage of*

any given project, but surely we don't have to take all day to do it? We should try issuing bulletins in advance, and then, when we do sit down together, we'll all be in the picture already, and can discuss the important points.

15 *Well, if I'd known it would be like this, I'd never have agreed to take it on in the first place. We should have set ourselves a target to start with, I suppose. Now it looks like we'll never get the job done. And the same thing's happening with other jobs, too. I want to see them finished up much quicker from now on, even if it means taking on extra staff in the short term.*

16 *It's only fair to expect a level playing field, and that's all I'm really suggesting. The present system's putting untold stress on some people, and leaving others under-employed. There's no reason why each branch should be trying to achieve a separate quota — it means some people are getting bonuses for what's only average for other people. We need to get everyone working on the same basis. I'm sure it'll improve productivity.*

17 *I hope we can manage to get things running better here. It's very frustrating, seeing so much inefficiency, and knowing what that's costing us. I really want to get everything better before we expand into the new premises. The problem lies in the way responsibilities are distributed among the various section heads, with each one separately doing their own accounts and payroll. I'd prefer to see that all handled centrally, done in a unified way.*

Section Two (CD Track 28)

18 *The journey should turn out to be worth it. They're obviously keen to do business with someone, and I just hope it'll be us. They seemed to like the samples I showed them, and said they thought our terms were fair. Of course actual details would get discussed later, but I'm hopeful they'll come on board, and it's a part of the world where we need customers. We'll have to see.*

19 *It was a long way to go, but of course it's necessary. We've had so many problems with components manufactured at that site. But as they were saying it's because the machinery was in need of replacement, then we had no choice but to go and check it out. It's true it's showing its age, but I think it's a question of repairs, not replacing it all. It'll take a few weeks, but then we should be back to normal.*

20 *I'm still not convinced I really needed to fly out — most of what we said could have been done by email or phone. After all, it's basically just a lot of figures, isn't it? But I guess because it will lead to important changes in our overall plans, it's better to sit down together and make sure we all agree on how to interpret the data. And some of the findings are really interesting.*

21 *Yes, not a bad trip, this time. And of course if we do decide to work together, then I won't have to come out nearly so often in the future. He seems to have the right background, and attitude, and some great contacts, so I'd be happy to have him as our man there. His office address is in a good part of town, and I think he'd be very likely to build up our customer base.*

22 *It's quite an event in itself, getting all the partners together — only happens about once a year. It's tough, trying to fit everything into a couple of days, especially when we'll be living with the decisions for a long time to come. But we have established a way forward, both targets and routes to meeting them. I think we'll be able to strengthen our market position this way, with new branches and customer growth.*

Part Three (CD Tracks 29–30)

M *Sally, everyone's talking about the changes. I'd be interested to know what you make of them.*

F *Well, Louis, I think it's a mixed bag. I guess they've been fairly carefully planned. I think every department head was consulted, so ideas were contributed from the whole organisation. The chairman put a lot of thought into bringing it all together, which is probably due to his background in consultancy — wanting to get the whole picture clear, before finally deciding.*

M *I hadn't realised they'd been so long in the making — they seemed to come out of the blue.*

F *Oh no, it's been building up. The idea is to give our whole operation a boost. We've been paying the price for low motivation for quite a while, and it's time to turn staff retention rates around. Sales and profits have been static for too long, but if we can get more commitment out of people, things should pick up.*

M *Sounds reasonable. As I say, I thought they'd happened rather suddenly. If other senior staff are thinking that too, they're going to feel some resentment. But then again, it doesn't mean they won't get on with implementing them, so I guess it'll all end up alright.*

F   I hope you're right. Still, I'm personally rather unconvinced about the new working hours.

M Oh?

F   Well the idea sounds nice – having core hours from 11 to 3 and leaving people free to start as early or late as they want and finish accordingly …

M And maybe working four long days and having longer weekends.

F   But it'll mean we'll be very understaffed on some days, and then those people who are here will have to take everybody's calls, so less actual work will get done – that's how I see it turning out in the end, anyway.

M I see what you mean. What other problems do you foresee?

F   I think the sales targets could have been better thought out. I know the idea is to encourage a spirit of healthy competition, which is no bad thing of course, but they've been applied right across the board in the departments affected. People can't be expected to achieve the same regardless of what they're selling. It's a fact that some models outsell others, and that ought to be reflected in the targets.

M Well, on a more positive note, I'm all in favour of the training that's being introduced.

F   Uh-huh.

M It's going to be far more accessible. When we had sessions provided by the college, the topics were rather limited, it seemed to me, but now there's a much wider range on offer, not just internet and database management all the time. I just hope they timetable it sensibly.

F   Oh, I think they will, after all the effort of setting it up. Something I'm looking forward to is the newsletter – that's a great idea.

M Yes, it makes you wonder why we haven't had one before.

F   It'll be a real boost for corporate culture, make everyone feel involved. The overseas reps will particularly appreciate it – they can feel outside the loop except when they're over here, which is only twice a year. I suppose most of the contributions will come from managers. People joining the company will probably assume we've always had it, but I'm sure it'll be an improvement.

M So, some hope for the future?

F   Let's give it about six months to see how it all plays out. It takes time to tell whether things are going to succeed, and everyone will need to be consulted to get their views and experiences on the changes. The real test will be morale, and whether it seems to go up or down, but I'd guess these won't be the last changes, and that we'll see more major changes introduced.

M As you say, time will tell …

ANSWER KEY

Practice Test 1

Preparation

Working out the meaning, Exercise 1

1 product, produce, production, productive, unproductive, producer, productivity, etc
2 employment, unemployment, employer, employee, employable, etc
3 competition, competitor, competitive, uncompetitive, etc
4 consumable, consumption, consumer, etc
5 different, differentiate, differentiation, differential, difference, etc

Working out the meaning, Exercise 2

1 productivity
2 employees
3 uncompetitive
4 consumer
5 differentiating

Grammar practice, Exercise 1

1 hearing
2 being asked to
3 spending
4 to make it easier
5 prices to / (that) prices will
6 to providing customers with
7 appreciate it if
8 for companies to merge / towards companies merging
9 to have left
10 you to

Grammar practice, Exercise 2

1 it
2 you
3 one/point
4 Another
5 also
6 It
7 These
8 Others/Some

Test 1: Reading

Part One

1 D   2 C   3 A   4 B   5 C   6 B   7 C

Part Two

8 F   9 D   10 A   11 E   12 C

Part Three

13 A   14 C   15 B   16 D   17 A   18 D

Part Four

19 D   20 C   21 A   22 C   23 B   24 A   25 D
26 B   27 B   28 A   29 D   30 B   31 C   32 C
33 A

Part Five

34 WHILE
35 OUT
36 SOON
37 FROM
38 ON
39 LOOK
40 GO
41 WHICH
42 CORRECT
43 IS
44 TO
45 CORRECT

Test 1: Writing

Part One (Sample answer)

Jerry – The delegation is due at 9.30 next Friday. They'll be interested in seeing the production plant, and I suggest you also take them to the R&D section. We'll have lunch at the Mermaid Hotel at 1 pm, and of course you're invited to join us.
Thanks
Susannah

Part Two (Sample answer)

To: Coralie Jenkins, Training Manager
From: Noel Roberts
Subject: TRAINING COURSE

I would like to attend the 'Introduction to management' training course which is described in the attached leaflet.

BENEFITS

The programme looks very useful, particularly the section on communication skills. This is because I am not very good at talking to other staff about poor standards of work.

The course includes work in small groups, and that is how I learn best. Hearing other people's ideas is stimulating.

Participants will be given notes on key topics. These will be handy, both for me and for some of my colleagues.

DATES

I would prefer to attend the September course, as I have arranged to take annual leave in July.

PRICE

There is a 5% price reduction for early booking, so I hope that you will agree to book the course for me before the end of May.

Test 1: Listening

Part One

1   PERSONNEL PRACTICE
2   PAY SYSTEMS
3   DECISION MAKING
4   ORGANISATIONAL CULTURE
5   INDUSTRIAL ANALYST
6   INSURANCE
7   RESEARCH
8   REGIONAL
9   TERMINAL TABLE
10 HEIGHT ADJUSTABLE
11 MOUSE SHELF
12 PRINTER STAND

Part Two

13 E   14 A   15 H   16 D   17 B
18 B   19 E   20 H   21 D   22 F

Part Three
23 A 24 C 25 B 26 B 27 C
28 A 29 C 30 C

Practice Test 2

Preparation

Working out the meaning, Exercise 1
1 D 2 E 3 C 4 A 5 B
6 G 7 F 8 B

Working out the meaning, Exercise 2
1 C 2 A 3 E 4 B 5 D

Grammar practice, Exercise 1
1 B 2 D 3 A 4 A 5 C 6 C

Grammar practice, Exercise 2
Other answers are also possible.
1 …as it keeps breaking down. /…because of its constant breakdowns.
2 …a 2% rise in its market share last year. / …its market share rise by 2% last year.
3 …was that it attracted new delegates. /…was the attendance of new delegates.
4 …sales rising by 10%. / …a 10% rise in sales.
5 …not only listening to what is said, but also noticing what is not said. / …both listening to what is said, and noticing what is not said.

Test 2: Reading

Part One
1 C 2 B 3 A 4 D 5 D 6 B 7 C

Part Two
8 E 9 B 10 F 11 A 12 D

Part Three
13 B 14 D 15 A 16 C 17 D 18 B

Part Four
19 C 20 B 21 A 22 A 23 B 24 D
25 D 26 C 27 B 28 A 29 C 30 C
31 A 32 B 33 D

Part Five
34	THAT	40	CORRECT
35	MUST	41	CORRECT
36	CORRECT	42	IF
37	IS	43	SUCH
38	THIS	44	AND
39	THEIR	45	ALTHOUGH

Test 2: Writing

Part One (Sample answer)

We're introducing the new staff suggestion scheme on 1 May. We want all staff to think about improvements to working conditions, productivity, customer relations, etc. Could you please email everyone about it, and tell them that suggestions should be put in the box in reception.
Thanks

Part Two (Sample answer)

To: Chris Sutcliffe, Managing Director
From: Lynn Dent
Subject: Performance in November

This report covers November's results in branches A-D, compared with those in October.

MONTHLY TURNOVER
Only branch A saw an improvement in turnover, which was probably the result of an advertising campaign in the local media. Neither branch B nor branch D reported any change, while in branch C turnover fell considerably.

STAFF TURNOVER
The only significant changes in staff turnover were in branches C and D. In C it rose sharply, from 2% to 8%, mainly because of dissatisfaction with the new manager. On the other hand, there was an improvement in branch D's previous high level of 10%.

SALES BY PRODUCT TYPE
Women's clothes, which are already the best selling goods, increased from 60 to 65% of total sales, at the expense of men's clothing. Children's clothes were unchanged, at 20%.

Test 2: Listening

Part One
1 LATEST CATALOGUE
2 IT CO-ORDINATOR
3 STRATEGY DOCUMENT
4 MARKET RESEARCH
5 CASE STUDIES
6 TEAMWORK
7 HANDOUT
8 HR SUPERVISOR
9 EXPORT SALES
10 COMMUNICATION SKILLS
11 PRESENTATION
12 SALES DIRECTOR

Part Two
13 D 14 A 15 E 16 H 17 C
18 E 19 H 20 G 21 C 22 B

Part Three
23 B 24 A 25 C 26 B 27 B
28 A 29 A 30 C

Practice Test 3

Preparation

Working out the meaning, Exercise 1

1 take over
2 speed up
3 revitalise
4 evaluate
5 combine

Grammar practice, Exercise 1

1 c 2 e 3 b 4 d 5 a

Possible paraphrase of 4: *This company is going to improve its stores.*

Grammar practice, Exercise 2

1 Explaining
2 Requesting action
3 Recommending
4 Predicting
5 Suggesting
6 Evaluating
7 Describing

Test 3: Reading

Part One

1 C 2 A 3 C 4 D 5 C 6 B 7 A

Part Two

8 E 9 D 10 A 11 F 12 C

Part Three

13 B 14 A 15 C 16 D 17 B 18 C

Part Four

19 C	20 B	21 A	22 B	23 D	24 C
25 A	26 D	27 A	28 D	29 B	30 B
31 C	32 C	33 D			

Part Five

34	THE	40	CORRECT
35	SO	41	FOR
36	IT	42	ONLY
37	THEIR	43	THERE
38	OF	44	AS
39	CORRECT	45	CORRECT

Test 3: Writing

Part One (Sample answer)

To support our strategy of growing sales in our Asian and African markets, a new position of assistant manager has been created. Paul Fisher has been appointed, and will start on 1st September. Paul has worked for several years in marketing toys, concentrating on the Far East.

Part Two (Sample answer)

Dear Ms Westgate

I am writing to ask if you might be interested in handling our advertising in Scotland.

We are a manufacturer of luxury kitchen units, which are sold through a number of retail chains in the south of England. We have now decided to launch our products in Scotland, as we believe there is a growing demand for quality goods like ours.

We are therefore looking for an agency which is familiar with the local media, to produce radio and newspaper advertising tailored to the Scottish market. We are keen to work very closely with the agency, to make sure that it understands our business philosophy. For this reason, it would be helpful if you could visit us at our head office.

I look forward to hearing from you.

Yours sincerely

Harry Clifton

Test 3: Listening

Part One

1 SCANNER
2 WIRELESS CABLE
3 AUTOMATIC TYPING
4 DEMONSTRATION DISKS
5 READER SURVEY
6 E-COMMERCE
7 LAY-OUT
8 COVER DESIGNS
9 IN-HOUSE TRAINING
10 SUGGESTION SCHEME
11 RECRUITMENT
12 DEVELOPMENT GROUP

Part Two

13 B	14 E	15 A	16 H	17 D
18 C	19 B	20 H	21 F	22 D

Part Three

23 C	24 A	25 B	26 A	27 C
28 B	29 C	30		

UNIVERSITY *of* CAMBRIDGE
Local Examinations Syndicate

V A N T A G E

Candidate Name
If not already printed, write name in CAPITALS and complete the Candidate No. grid (in pencil).

Candidate's Signature

Examination Title

Centre

Supervisor:
If the candidate is ABSENT or has WITHDRAWN shade here ▭

Centre No.

Candidate No.

Examination Details

0	0	0	0
1	1	1	1
2	2	2	2
3	3	3	3
4	4	4	4
5	5	5	5
6	6	6	6
7	7	7	7
8	8	8	8
9	9	9	9

BEC Vantage Reading Answer Sheet

Instructions
Use a PENCIL (B or HB).
Rub out any answer you wish to change with an eraser.

For **Parts 1 to 4:**
Mark one box for each answer.

For example:
If you think C is the right answer to the question, mark your answer sheet like this:

0	A	B	C

For **Part 5:**
Write your answer clearly in CAPITAL LETTERS.
Write one letter in each box.

For example:

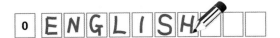

| 0 | E | N | G | L | I | S | H | | | |

Part 1

1	A	B	C	D
2	A	B	C	D
3	A	B	C	D
4	A	B	C	D
5	A	B	C	D
6	A	B	C	D
7	A	B	C	D

Part 2

8	A	B	C	D	E	F	G
9	A	B	C	D	E	F	G
10	A	B	C	D	E	F	G
11	A	B	C	D	E	F	G
12	A	B	C	D	E	F	G

Turn over for Parts 3 - 5 ▶

Part 3

13	A	B	C	D
14	A	B	C	D
15	A	B	C	D
16	A	B	C	D
17	A	B	C	D
18	A	B	C	D

Part 4

19	A	B	C	D
20	A	B	C	D
21	A	B	C	D
22	A	B	C	D
23	A	B	C	D
24	A	B	C	D
25	A	B	C	D
26	A	B	C	D

27	A	B	C	D
28	A	B	C	D
29	A	B	C	D
30	A	B	C	D
31	A	B	C	D
32	A	B	C	D
33	A	B	C	D

Part 5

34		1 34 0
35		1 35 0
36		1 36 0
37		1 37 0
38		1 38 0
39		1 39 0
40		1 40 0
41		1 41 0
42		1 42 0
43		1 43 0
44		1 44 0
45		1 45 0

UNIVERSITY *of* CAMBRIDGE
Local Examinations Syndicate

V A N T A G E

Candidate Name
If not already printed, write name in CAPITALS and complete the Candidate No. grid (in pencil).

Candidate's Signature

Examination Title

Centre

Supervisor:
If the candidate is ABSENT or has WITHDRAWN shade here ▭

Centre No.

Candidate No.

Examination Details

0	0	0	0
1	1	1	1
2	2	2	2
3	3	3	3
4	4	4	4
5	5	5	5
6	6	6	6
7	7	7	7
8	8	8	8
9	9	9	9

BEC Vantage Listening Answer Sheet

Instructions
Use a PENCIL (B or HB).
Rub out any answer you wish to change with an eraser.

For **Part 1:**
Write your answer clearly in CAPITAL LETTERS.
Write one letter or number in each box.
If the answer has more than one word, leave one box empty between words.

For example:

 0 QUESTION 12

For **Parts 2 and 3:**
Mark one box for each answer.

For example:
If you think C is the right answer to the question, mark your answer sheet like this:

0 A B C̲

Part 1 - Conversation One

1

1 1 0

2

1 2 0

3

1 3 0

4

1 4 0

▭ Continue on the other side of this sheet ▶

Part 1 - Conversation Two

5 [ ]

1 5 0

6 [ ]

1 6 0

7 [ ]

1 7 0

8 [ ]

1 8 0

Part 1 - Conversation Three

9 [ ]

1 9 0

10 [ ]

1 10 0

11 [ ]

1 11 0

12 [ ]

1 12 0

Part 2 - Section One

13	A	B	C	D	E	F	G	H
14	A	B	C	D	E	F	G	H
15	A	B	C	D	E	F	G	H
16	A	B	C	D	E	F	G	H
17	A	B	C	D	E	F	G	H

Part 2 - Section Two

18	A	B	C	D	E	F	G	H
19	A	B	C	D	E	F	G	H
20	A	B	C	D	E	F	G	H
21	A	B	C	D	E	F	G	H
22	A	B	C	D	E	F	G	H

Part 3

23	A	B	C
24	A	B	C
25	A	B	C
26	A	B	C
27	A	B	C
28	A	B	C
29	A	B	C
30	A	B	C